Housing for the Elderly

**Institute of
Real Estate
Management
Monographs**

Series on
Specific Property
Types

Each monograph in this series focuses on the management and related aspects of a specific type of property. Each monograph is written and reviewed by the leading experts on the type of property concerned, and is thorough and authoritative. *Housing for the Elderly: The Handbook for Managers* is one monograph in this series.

The Institute of Real Estate Management (IREM) of the NATIONAL ASSOCIATION OF REALTORS® is an organization of professional property managers that certifies property managers who have distinguished themselves in the areas of education, experience, and ethical conduct. IREM offers property managers and the public an expansive program of courses, seminars, books, periodicals, audiovisual kits, and other educational activities and materials. INSTITUTE OF REAL ESTATE MANAGEMENT MONOGRAPHS: SERIES ON SPECIFIC PROPERTY TYPES was created as part of this professional program.

Keith F. Levine,

Publishing Manager

Betty T. Moore,

Project Editor

Housing for the Elderly

The Handbook for Managers

Rosetta E. Parker, CPM®

IREM

Institute of Real Estate Management
of the NATIONAL ASSOCIATION OF REALTORS®
430 North Michigan Avenue, Chicago, Illinois 60611-4090

International Standard Book Number: 0-912104-68-6
Library of Congress Catalog Card Number: 83-81942

Printed in the United States of America

Preface

In no other form of property management is there so great an opportunity to relate directly to individual needs and elevate the quality of life for residents as in the management of housing for the elderly. I have found that this makes the role of manager of housing for the elderly uniquely challenging and gratifying. For example, new residents who no longer have their families and friends with them may look to the housing manager as their first link with the community inside and outside the complex. Those who have chronic ailments or disabilities and those who have lost a family member on whom they have been dependent are particularly vulnerable. The manager's role involves more than providing them with a place to live; it is an opportunity to allay any fears connected with retirement living, to establish a mutually beneficial relationship, and to introduce these residents to a new and satisfying way of life that can extend many years into the future. The creation of such a community is a product of the highest level of professionalism in the property manager's role.

Housing for the Elderly: The Handbook for Managers is the first comprehensive text to set forth the specific professional property management techniques and procedures involved in serving tenants who are elderly—with regard to the range of abilities and disabilities found in this group. The minimum age for Social Security retirement benefits—62—is the criterion used in this work in characterizing these individuals as elderly. The elderly population includes a large number of persons who are healthy, vigorous, active, and independent, a large number whose health and ability to be independent fluctuates, and a smaller number with disabilities that require physical supports and services on a continuing basis. One of the aims of this book is to provide methods of integrating these three groups within a housing complex that serves the needs of all, at the same time preserving the safety, dignity and greatest possible degree of independence of these individuals. The idea of incorporating physical supports such as grab rails as standard equipment for all dwelling units in the complex has startled some housing planners who presupposed the costs to be prohibitive; chapter 8 presents evidence to the contrary. Ingenuity and awareness of sources can achieve access to needed services economically, as this chapter demonstrates. The effect of success in such an effort is the ability to accommodate the changing needs of these tenants through many years of residence in the complex.

In addition to providing me with many of the problem-solving approaches and strategies you will find in these pages, the years I have spent—more than 15—in the management of housing for the elderly have been profoundly rewarding in terms of developing new values and criteria for achievement— and in terms of the human relationships they have brought into my life. In addition, sharing these experiences with other specialists in this type of management has revealed new insights, perspectives, and resources.

In order to render this handbook as intelligible and useful as possible to all persons connected with the planning and operation of housing for the elderly—property managers, as well as designers, architects, administrators, builders, financial officers, sponsors, and others—technical terms from each of these areas have been kept to a minimum. Terms without an equivalent term in general usage are defined as they are used in the text.

The tremendous increase in numbers of the elderly populace, and the prospect of even sharper increases in the years to come, indicate the urgency of the need for additional housing, and the need to equip many additional property management professionals with these specialized skills. The waiting lists for such housing are already lengthy; government and community "hotlines" are crowded with calls. This handbook can be used as a practical guide for managers new to the field, in conjunction with the basic property management texts published by the Institute of Real Estate Management. For those who are familiar with the fundamentals of property management, this book is presented as a comprehensive, detailed analysis of the needs to be served and the many creative uses of resources to be made in fulfilling the role of manager of housing for the elderly.

Rosetta E. Parker, CPM®
1984

Acknowledgments

In bringing together the multiplicity of elements pertinent to the compassionate and efficient management of housing for the elderly, it has been necessary to tap the resources of literally hundreds of individual experts, public housing finance agencies, housing authorities, and groups devoted to business, consumer and public interest. These groups are listed in Appendix A, the published works in the Bibliography. Only a few of the individuals and organizations to whom I owe a debt of gratitude for ideas and information presented here can be listed in the space available; I wish to express my thanks to all.

I have had the privilege of being associated with the Virginia Housing Development Authority (Richmond, Virginia), whose leadership in developing multifamily units through its network of sponsors provided me with thousands of units' worth of experience in this type of management. Other management companies contributing substantially to this body of information are: Fellowship Foundation, Reston, Virginia; Pemberton Management Company, Boston, Massachusetts; Shannon & Luchs Company, Specialized Housing Division, Washington, D.C.; and The John Stewart Company, Sausalito, California.

The North Carolina Department of Insurance has granted permission to reprint pages containing diagrams, specifications, and illustrations from *Accessible Housing: A Manual on North Carolina's Building Code Requirements for Accessible Housing*, published by the Special Office for the Handicapped, Insurance Commissioner's Office, North Carolina Department of Insurance, 1980 (all rights reserved); these pages appear in chapter 7 of this book. Permission to reprint excerpts from a resident's handbook has been received from the Pleasant View Home, Broadway, Virginia; these excerpts appear in chapter 4. Among the housing complexes contributing information are: Hilliard (Chicago Housing Authority); The Lewinsville Retirement Residence, Inc., McLean, Virginia; Lutheran Home and Service for the Aged, Arlington Heights, Illinois; Morningside Court, Chicago; and Mei Lun Yuen, San Francisco.

Joan A. Pease, Partners in Planning, Washington, D.C., consultant in retirement housing and health care environments, photographed the Lewinsville facilities shown in the first and second chapters. The U.S. Department of Housing and Urban Development has given permission to print photographs of facilities in several geographical locations. Valued resources and guidance have been provided by Beverly F. Dordick, librarian for the NATIONAL ASSOCIATION OF REALTORS®, Chicago. The library of Grace Lutheran Church, River Forest, Illinois, has contributed to the historical background and widened current perspectives on the practical exercise of compassion in the management of elderly housing.

Some of the supportive features discussed in chapter 7 have been subtly incorporated into the design of Morningside Court. Visible in the entrance shown on the cover of this book in a photograph taken by Bruce Mitzit, architectural photographer, Chicago, are a gently sloped ramp recessed from the street, nonslip tile flooring, hand grips and continuous wooden hand rails, and nonglare lighting including lighted exit signs. A glass wall separates the locked foyer, which contains a security system telephone, from the inner hallway and manager's office. Above the doorway is an overhang, with recessed nonglare lighting, that functions as a protective canopy. The design of the cover of the book itself, as well as the design of the inside pages of the book, is the work of Harry Voigt, Oak Park, Illinois.

A special note of thanks is due to the property management professionals whose judgment and care in reviewing the manuscript for accuracy and thoroughness has lent added authority to this work: Donald M. Furbush, CPM®, BankAmerica Realty Services, Inc., San Francisco; Dorothy Rose Gagnier, doctoral candidate in educational gerontology, University of Michigan, Ann Arbor; Jeanne P. Kinnard, housing coordinator, American Association of Homes for the Aging, Washington, D.C.; Joan I. Maas, CPM®, regional vice president–direct management, Security Pacific, Inc., Northbrook, Illinois; and Penny Tourangeau, CPM®, The John Stewart Company, Sausalito, California.

I am particularly grateful to Keith F. Levine, publishing manager of IREM, for his invaluable work in coordinating the project and bringing it to fulfillment, and to Betty T. Moore, project editor, for her thoroughgoing professionalism in shaping the narrative and illustrations into a complete, yet succinct, program for excellence in management that is eminently usable by managers at all levels to meet current and future elderly housing needs.

R. E. P.

Contents

3 The Manager's Role / 17

4 Managing the Housing Process / 29

8   Finances and Asset Management / 85

Dedicated in appreciation
to all property managers, social workers,
gerontologists and clergy who serve
senior citizens and the handicapped
R. E. P.

1 Housing Needs of Elderly Persons

The creation of housing for the elderly concentrates a population with special needs—physical, social and financial—into one community. To identify these needs and their variations among individual residents, and to find the optimum means to fulfill them within the context of sound management practices, are ongoing challenges for the property manager.

The Growing Need for Qualified Managers

The key to success in providing housing for elderly persons is good management—the catalyst that brings together trained professional talents and the architectural design features that best serve the residents, under an administration furnishing adequate means to support the project.

For the growing number of housing complexes devoted to persons of retirement age, there are relatively few managers who have the specialized training this work requires. That is perhaps the weakest link in the delivery system of housing for the elderly. The demand for qualified managers is expected to remain substantial, and even to increase, as more and more units are built to house the burgeoning retirement-age population.

Currently, close to 12 percent of the population of the United States can be considered to be of retirement age according to the criterion set by the Social Security Administration: age 62 and beyond. That proportion is expected to grow beyond 13 percent by the year 2000, and beyond 21 percent by 2030. For the first time, the retirement-age population outnumbers teenagers; it is greater than the total number of persons who have ever lived to age 62 or beyond.

Changes in the Elderly Population

At retirement age today, people are typically healthier, better-educated, and more active than previous generations have been. Advances in medical care and in the general standard of living enable many to live vastly longer lives than their forbears. The average life expectancy of persons born in 1900 was 47 years. This was based partially on a high rate of infant mortality, but also it

1

was relatively rare for a person to survive beyond the sixth decade. For persons born in 1984, average life expectancy is considered to be close to 75 years. It is true that this figure represents a sharp reduction in infant mortality, but also it is now not uncommon for persons to live into their 80s and 90s. In a number of housing complexes for the elderly, the average age of the residents is between 82 and 83.

It is not surprising, then, to find that already the number of housing complexes designed for elderly persons has fallen behind the demand, and the waiting lists for these units are long. Development of an equitable system for setting priorities among these applicants has become a necessity for the managers of these properties.

Housing for the elderly is, perhaps, unique in its involvement of the manager in understanding and monitoring individual residents' current and changing life situations. Especially for those advanced in age who may have survived their families and friends, changes in health or financial status can constitute crises that call for action on the part of the property manager. But at all times, success in managing these properties is predicated on the ability to supply the affordable housing features and services that represent the tenants' desires and needs. In order to provide managers with the essential decision-making tools, it is necessary to explore the special needs of retirement-age persons and the housing alternatives that can be considered.

Special Needs of Elderly Persons

To consider the needs persons of retirement age have in common is not to imply that aging eliminates or even modifies their individuality.

If anything, the effect of different experiences, life-styles, and economic opportunities endure and accumulate over time, so that those who are the elderly may be the least homogeneous age group within the population (Raymond J. Struyk, Beth J. Soldo, and Carol DeVita, *Improving the Elderly's Housing* [Cambridge, Mass.: Ballinger Publishing Company, 1980], p. 15).

The physical, social and financial needs of elderly persons do not differ from those of other age groups altogether as a result of the aging process; there are powerful environmental influences that can shape these needs.

The Concept of Retirement Age

Retirement age as a concept did not exist before the late 1880s, when Chancellor Otto von Bismarck of Prussia established a life pension for all workers reaching age 65. Because life expectancy at that time was 47 years, on the average, it was contemplated that this reform would win votes for Bismarck without costing the government an excessive amount. Workers saw the pension as protection from poverty in old age. Observing this strategy, Benjamin Disraeli, as prime minister, started the system in Great Britain. In 1935 the United States Social Security Administration was instituted, making retirement benefits available at 65; later, the minimum age was lowered to 62.

With longevity increasing dramatically, and an inflationary economy reducing the buying power of fixed incomes, retirement, for vast numbers of persons, has become a period of hardship. Social Security funding has become precarious. Legislators have drawn up plans to raise the age of eligibility for Social Security pension payments. Some companies have eliminated compulsory retirement.

All would live long, but none would be old (Beatrice and Ira Freeman).

The most widespread and devastating effect of the retirement-age concept has been the change in public attitude toward persons in this age group, with a resulting change in their self-esteem. Retirement age has come to be accepted as a time of lowered expectations for acuity, achievement, and worth to the community, in the experience of many. In the areas of the world noted for longevity—Ecuador's Vilcabamba Valley, Pakistan's Valley of the Hanza, and the U.S.S.R's Caucasus Mountains—researchers have found that elderly residents sustain a sense of well-being through continued participation in community chores and activities. Amish communities provide for voluntary, gradual reduction of work expectations, without a loss of status. In all these areas, respect for elderly persons is traditional. A Louis Harris survey reports that 73 percent of Americans 65 and over prefer to continue working rather than to accept the reductions in status, income, and expectations that are the lot of many who retire. Of the 55-to-64 age group, the percentage of those anticipating working beyond the established retirement age is even higher. Upon compulsory retirement, many have begun "retirement" careers, some out of financial necessity, others out of the need for meaningful use of their energies and talents.

Even for those persons who look forward to retirement as a "natural" concomitant of the aging process, and welcome the opportunity for leisure time, there is a need for a period of orientation to these changes in life-style, pace, and community status.

The manager's sensitivity to elderly residents' needs for status, mainstream activity, and a period of adjustment can be amplified through a study of levels of aging within the group. Bernice L. Neugarten, past president of the Gerontological Society, has outlined changes in the stereotypes of the elderly population ("Age Groups in American Society and the Rise of the Young-Old," *Annals of the American Academy* [1975], p. 187). She characterizes the "young-old" as between 55 and 75, relatively healthy, relatively affluent, relatively free from traditional responsibilities of work and family, increasingly well educated and politically active; this group, she believes, has "enormous potential as agents of social change in creating an age-irrelevant society and in thus improving the relations between age groups." This "young-old" group constitutes some 15 percent of the total population of the United States, as contrasted with the "old-old" group—75 years and up—who represent about 4 percent of the total population. Most of the "young-old" group, with relatively few limitations related to health, can live independently. They think of age-segregated housing in terms of the range of options it offers for self-enhancement and meaningful community participation. Some need the option of caring for an aged ("old-old") parent in the dwelling-place. In contrast to the "young-old," the "old-old"—the smallest but fastest-growing segment of fastest-growing group in the total population—have incomes averaging around or below poverty level. Many of the "old-old" need more supportive social services and special features in the physical environment as health-related problems develop among them. Their options for employment are severely restricted, as are their options for social contacts and other meaningful activities. The resourceful property manager who has sufficient insight into their needs can contribute to the quality of their lives by enhancing the quality of the housing facility and services. Improved morale and health, and lengthened lifespan and residence in the facility can result.

Physical Needs

A study of 2,000 elderly revealed that conditions considered by the elderly themselves to be age-related were diagnosed by their physicians as treatable disease. Absent medical surveillance allows the possibility that potentially reversible conditions will go untreated, resulting in permanent disability and dependency. Nevertheless, the majority of the elderly, including those with serious medical conditions, are able to function with minimal supports in the

HUD

Helping residents get to know one another

community. An important recent development is public housing for the well elderly providing architectural modification to facilitate functioning (no sills, emergency alarm buttons, and common spaces for social activities). Barrier-free housing is recognized as important in maintaining independent functioning. The less energy required to negotiate the environment, the easier it is to function despite physical impairment (Richard W. Besdine and Sylvia Sherwood, "Health-Care Needs of Elderly in Congregate Housing," *Congregate Housing for Older People* [Lexington, Mass.: D.C. Heath & Co., 1982], page 197).

Chronic and acute illness and disability can happen at any time in life, but in managing housing facilities for the elderly these problems must be considered as eventualities. In a typical modern urban housing complex designed for independent living, two apartments on each floor are equipped with special features for residents who are disabled in some way. Many buildings, especially older ones, have no such facilities; the property managers responsible for them face difficult decisions when residents experience temporary or permanent disabilities. Communication suffers when residents who fear that they will no longer be allowed to keep their apartments are reluctant to let the manager know of difficulties they are having. Some do not seek treatment until the condition becomes serious. Decisions to equip residential buildings with special features making it possible for individuals who have various degrees of disability to function independently should be considered as early as possible in the planning stages for new construction or for renovation or conversion of older buildings. A point in favor of incorporating these special features into housing for the elderly is that, on the whole, residents who are physically fit also welcome these conveniences. Another is that these features will make it possible for established residents to remain as tenants despite changes that may occur as they age. Details of these features are shown and discussed in chapter 7. Basic physical needs related to architectural and design considerations include the need for good circulation of air in the building to minimize difficulties in breathing, for easy access and

Pease

Caution signs on glass doors, unlocked by buzzer signal system; hand rails extending from front door into entrance hall, within reach of supportive easy chairs; lighted ceilings and signs; nonslip flooring; posted activity schedules, and reception desk phone provide security and comfort.

egress, for safety bars at bathtubs and other possible danger points, and for protection from hazards.

Social Needs

Women far outnumber men in the retirement-age category. The ratio is something like 146 women to each 100 men in current population figures. Most women marry men older than themselves. On the average, women outlive men of the same age by about eight years. These facts combine to explain the fact that the preponderance of residents in housing for the elderly are widows, and most of the male residents are married. Moreover, reports Joan I. Maas, CPM®, Chicago, "Male participation in social activities in elderly housing always seems to be far less successful than female participation. Disengagement, or withdrawal from community life, in male retirees is far more prevalent, and therefore staff must be aware of this particular situation."

Loneliness is rated as a "very serious" problem among residents whose lives have been uprooted by loss. It is important for a manager to recognize and remedy these residents' "calls for help" that may come in many forms: requests to check on fixtures or equipment or complaints about health, for example—by helping residents get to know one another through social interaction within the complex. Managerial sensitivity to their predicament has come a long way since the public housing policy established in 1937 that allowed elderly persons to occupy units for low-income families only as couples. Until 1956, policy dictated that if one died, the remaining spouse had to vacate the unit within 30 days.

Security is a deep concern of elderly persons. Many who are otherwise able to remain in their homes and live independently choose to enter housing for the elderly in order to free themselves from the threat of crime or harassment that they fear has made their neighborhoods unsafe. Such persons are among the first applicants for elderly housing they see being constructed or converted in these same neighborhoods. They look for tangible means of protection. Most do not wish to leave the neighborhood that has become familiar to them over the years; they simply wish to live in a building that offers an extra measure of protection against crime.

Another type of security desired is to get away from the barriers and other physical features of their homes or neighborhoods that, as a consequence of sensory or motor impairment, constitute hazards for them. The opportunity to obtain the needed architectural features and some housekeeping assistance and other services in a housing complex enables them to function with relative independence rather than to be confined to their living quarters and have to hire someone to help them, or, perhaps, to have to enter a nursing home for full-time care when only part-time assistance is needed.

Financial and Other Needs

For most of the elderly population, the primary need is for financial support of essential housing; some support has come from nonprofit organizations and government subsidies, and more is needed. Management is also challenged to provide desired facilities and services such as recreational equipment, educational programs and social events, along with appropriate safety and health features and a means of monitoring changes in residents' needs. From time to time, a manager may need to provide consumer guidance, help with money management, and tips on part-time and full-time employment at home or in the area.

Housing Alternatives for the Elderly

The idea of devoting special housing to elderly persons originated, in the United States, during the nineteenth century, within religious congregations, who, at first, sheltered and cared for the needy aged, and for orphaned children, under one roof. Old and young reached out to each other for comfort and care, deriving a sense of family life that is more difficult to achieve within a single age group. Increased funding from religious and community organizations, and eventually from the government, made it possible to create special housing for the elderly, and fund foster care for children, but research has confirmed the benefits to be derived from frequent multigenerational socializing. In the absence of such opportunities within the resident's family, community organizations in many areas develop visitation programs and events that foster mutually beneficial relationships.

Aging in Place

At least 75 percent of retirement-age persons own their homes; most of the others are renters. The majority prefer to remain where they are rather than relocate to a retirement community or housing complex, as long as they can function independently. Despite the fact that it is the minority of persons in the retirement years who constitute the market for elderly housing, the size of that market must be gauged in terms of the fast growth in numbers of this age group. For example, the U.S. Census of 1980 counted more than 25 million persons of retirement age—double the figure for 1950, and less than half the figure projected for the year 2000.

For owners and renters alike, the costs of remaining in their homes increase with the years. Shelter costs currently run 30 to 35 percent of their average income (in taxes and maintenance costs for owners; in rental rate increases and maintenance costs for renters). As they and their dwelling-places age, more assistance is needed from community and government sources in order to maintain the property. Many decide, as they arrive at the "old-old" level, that health and safety considerations dictate a move to housing that better serves their needs.

Home Sharing

Some elderly persons are able to remain in their homes longer because they choose to share them with others. Two or three widows, for instance, might share a house or apartment rather than bear the expense and labor of maintaining separate dwellings. Another type of home sharing is exemplified by the experience of a religious congregation that acquired a 10-room apartment in an older building and renovated it to provide separate bedrooms for several elderly parishioners, who shared the kitchen facilities, living and dining areas, and the chores.

Extended Household/ Echo Housing/Granny Flats

Members of several generations of some families arrange to occupy separate portions of the same dwelling-place, for example, a duplex, triplex, or separate houses on the same tract of land. In Australia, the government erects a prefabricated dwelling, called a "granny flat," in a family-owned area such as the back yard, rents it out to a family member as long as the need exists, and then removes it. This concept has been brought to the United States in the form of private enterprise, and renamed "echo housing" to remove the age stigma associated with the word "granny," but as a form of more or less temporary housing, it has come into conflict with zoning laws in some areas.

Modular Homes/Mobile Homes

Some persons of retirement age who seek to simplify their lifestyles and reduce the cost of living sell their homes or terminate their leases and move into smaller quarters such as a modular home or mobile home. In many instances, this decision coincides with relocation to a climate offering milder weather or an area that has vacation-spot amenities. Particularly in trailer parks, but also in areas where modular housing is permitted, zoning difficulties and limited accessibility of shopping and service facilities are drawbacks. If, as the years advance, health problems arise, the difficulties can become insurmountable.

Retirement Residences

Apartment houses and apartment hotels in many areas have been converted into residences for persons of retirement age and "preretirement age" (starting at 50 or 55) who can live independently but appreciate the security and convenience of a retiree-oriented building and the opportunity for companionship with peers. The typical retirement residence is a single high-rise building with efficiency or studio apartments and one-bedroom apartments; many of these have some apartments equipped with special features for disabled or handicapped tenants. Chapter 7 provides details of these special features. The total number of units is typically fewer than 500. The building has at least one small and one large communal room where meetings, social events, and adult education classes may be held. In resort areas and vacation spots, retirement residences come equipped with amenities such as swimming pools and tennis courts. Units typical of these areas have balconies or small private patios.

Retirement Communities

Towns, villages, and subdivisions have been created for the retirement-age population, and for those in the preretirement category. In the towns, and, to a lesser extent, in the villages, housing, in a middle-to-upper price bracket, is available in many forms: apartments, low-rise buildings, duplexes, triplexes, and quadriplexes. The towns are self-contained entities with medical, financial, recreational, and shopping facilities close to residential areas. Most retirement villages are situated next to existing urban or suburban centers of activity. A subdivision is a planned residential area within a pre-existing community affording the needed amenities. It provides a dwelling place—a single-family house or space to park a mobile home—and, in addition, usually a community building that functions as a meeting-place and recreation center.

Group Homes

A group home is part of a system of community-based residential dwellings with the resources to help elderly handicapped or disabled persons develop their potential to live independently. These resources include special architectural features and built-in furnishings such as those shown in chapter 7 of this book.

Congregate Housing

Congregate housing offers private living quarters with access to the services needed by persons not totally independent, yet not in need of nursing care. Each apartment has a kitchen or kitchenette, but there is also a central kitchen and dining room serving those who do not wish to cook any or all of their meals. Social and other supportive services are provided within the complex, or made accessible. Activities are organized; some residents run small businesses, such as craft and gift shops or cleaning services, on the premises. A variety of levels of needs for service can be accommodated, with the flexibility to provide for service changes when needs increase or, as sometimes happens, diminish. The latter has been observed in cases where depression resulting from an individual's difficulty in coping with an environment that has become uncomfortable has rendered the person relatively inactive. Moving from that environment into congregate housing that answers that individual's need can eventually result in increasing the individual's feeling of capability and usefulness, and help relieve or eliminate the feelings of depression. This, in turn, can spur the person to make new efforts toward independence. Congregate housing thus varies in the constellation of services offered and utilized by residents. The ability to foresee and provide for future needs of tenants is especially important to sponsors and planners of congregate housing and lifecare facilities (also called "continuing-care communities").

Lifecare Facilities

The concept of lifecare can be applied to a retirement community of any kind, but most often means a retirement village or high-rise building or buildings with a health care center. Some facilities charge a simple monthly rental. Others require a lump sum endowment plus a monthly rental. Still others require only the endowment. Some lifecare contracts place the person's assets in the care of management. Other contracts provide for the lifecare facility to take over the assets, which then may become the property of management. In return, the management provides the resident with a dwelling place—most often, an apartment or shared house—for the rest of the resident's life, and also provides health care as needs arise. Many lifecare facilities have a nursing home on the premises. Patients who become acutely ill are transferred to a nearby hospital. Upon the death of a resident, some lifecare facilities, especially those sponsored by religious groups, provide for funeral services. Some provide legal services, including asset management and administration of the will. Other services, such as the availability of hot meals and part-time homemaker, and resources such as transportation to shopping areas and recreation centers, are included in the contract. Lifecare typically assures the resident of lifelong shelter and care regardless of the number of years involved and the state of the resident's financial resources. About 600 lifecare/continuing-care retirement communities are in operation, and 1,000 to 1,500 are to be established by 1990 to meet the growing needs of the elderly who are in middle and upper-middle income brackets, according to a 1983 survey by Laventhol & Horwath, a national public accounting and consulting company.

Nursing Homes

Persons whose needs for health care are continuous, but not acute, may be accommodated in nursing homes, which provide two levels of care. These levels are classified as *intermediate*—help with the routines of living, such as getting up, walking, taking medication, and personal grooming—and *skilled*—round-the-clock nursing care. Fewer than 5 percent of the elderly live in nursing homes at any one time, but about 20 percent eventually enter one, at 84, on the average. Upon dismissal from a hospital when the acute stage of a serious illness has passed, an elderly person may be cared for at home by family members, who may be assisted by a local hospice organization. The alternative often selected is a nursing home. According to a U.S. Senate report, studies of the characteristics and needs of the nursing home population in the United States, indicate that 15 to 20 percent of the persons in nursing homes are misplaced, having been forced into these institutions "simply because public programs could not give attention to alternative ways of meeting their needs outside of an institution." Of the 20,000 nursing homes in the United States, 6 percent are owned and operated by the federal government, mainly through the Veterans Administration. Community agencies and religious and fraternal groups operate 20 percent of these homes, on a nonprofit basis. The remaining 74 percent, privately-owned, must make a profit in order to remain in operation. Although there are many fine examples of compassionately-managed and well-equipped nursing homes in the private sector as well as in the nonprofit category, the Subcommittee on Long-Term Care of the Special Committee on Aging of the U.S. Senate has reported that the majority fail to meet standards of acceptability. John M. Mason, consultant to agencies of care for the aged, describes these homes as "warehouses of the living dead," citing (*The Fourth Generation* [Minneapolis, Minn.: Augsburg Publishing House, 1978], p. 197) "sedation therapy" as an example of a common abuse: borderline patients are kept sedated so that they will need the skilled care that brings in additional funds through the Medicare and Medicaid programs. No funds are earmarked to support programs to help these persons recover.

Management Needs

This book is concerned with the many aspects of the property manager's role in the day-to-day administration and operation of retirement residences, retirement communities and lifecare facilities. Whether they are operated on a nonprofit or for-profit basis, and whether they are privately or publicly-sponsored, these dwelling places largely shape the future lives of those who have reached retirement age—the fastest-growing segment of the population. The property manager who has the training and background to be aware of these residents' changing needs, and is able to meet them within the perspective of good business practice, not only contributes to the quality of the residents' lives but also becomes a bulwark to the continuing function and success of the property.

The chapters that follow describe functions common to the management of a variety of housing on the three basic levels of service to the retirement-age population:

1. Independent living.
2. Semi-independent living.
3. Supported living.

The details and examples in the following chapters should provide sufficient working knowledge to enable the property manager to acquire some experience in this specialized field.

2   Sponsorship and Management

The owner or sponsor providing the financial backing for a housing complex for the elderly, as the moving force behind the project, represents an interest that should be involved throughout the operating phase as well as in the planning stages. In most nonprofit projects, a board of directors provides guidance for the development and management of the property. Policies are set according to the organization's principles and purposes, which commonly are available in written form in the organization's charter or other basic documents. Among projects operating on a for-profit basis, many leave it to the manager to set policy and make decisions as the need arises. Where this is the case, the manager can base decisions on the sponsor's stated goals in acquiring the property. In the process of housing the elderly, where it is necessary to cope with many inequities, there is a special need for fairness, firmness, and consistency, in setting policies and priorities, to facilitate day-to-day decision making.

Private Sponsorship

Some examples of sponsors of housing for the elderly in the private sector are: nonprofit organizations, such as church groups, hospitals, universities, and groups devoted to the interests of the retirement-age population; charitable organizations such as Volunteers of America, the Salvation Army, veterans' groups, and societies serving handicapped persons; and conventional sponsors, such as financial institutions; and housing development groups.

Typically, in the case of a nonprofit or charitable organization, a subsidiary is formed and formally incorporated. A tax exemption is applied for under Internal Revenue Code 501 (c)(3), to enable the subsidiary to fund the project through donations and bequests. A board is elected or appointed, and a professional with experience in housing for the elderly—preferably a CERTIFIED PROPERTY MANAGER® (CPM®)—is hired to work with the development team. The latter usually consists of at least one staff executive from the sponsoring organization, plus an attorney, an architect, a contractor, a representative of a financial institution or firm, and the real estate professional/CPM®.

Conventional sponsors and housing development groups in the private sector work in much the same way, except that their financial or housing development expertise comes from their own organizations rather than being engaged by a volunteer organization, and funding is already earmarked for the project. However, few such housing projects are brought to fruition without some reference to public funding; virtually all receive some assistance, direct or indirect—few such projects can support the full burden of taxation. The sponsor must apply to the government for abatement of taxes. Local resistance to a tax-exempt project—as a use for the property that takes it off the tax rolls—may emerge as imposition of a zoning restriction not easily waived. For these and other reasons the team works best when each member has had prior experience in developing housing for the elderly.

Public Sponsorship

Federal government sponsorship of dwelling-places for low-income families was established by the 1937 U.S. Housing Act combining federal financing with local responsibility. In 1956, when elderly persons occupied 10 percent of these units, Congress passed legislation opening public housing to elderly single persons and making elderly housing eligible for Federal Housing Administration (FHA) 207 mortgage insurance. In 1958 the first public housing project planned specifically for the elderly was completed. The National Housing Act of 1959 made the Housing and Urban Development (HUD) 202 direct loan program available to nonprofit sponsors of housing for elderly persons with low or moderate incomes; revised in 1974, it provides direct 40-year financing to nonprofit sponsors for construction or renovation of such housing. The White House Conference on Aging, in 1971, recommended allocating federal, state, and local government funds sufficient for the construction and opening of 120,000 new units per year. That goal has not been met. The Housing and Community Development Act of 1974 replaced a number of categorical grant programs with community development block grants, and included, in Section 8, a program of rental assistance payments on behalf of low-income residents of new, existing, or renovated units. In 1975, HUD provided for permanent financing for the 202 program. By 1984, elderly persons occupied about half the public housing in the United States.

The Sponsor's Role

Goal-setting is a fundamental task of the sponsor. The goals set for the project must be based on the current and future needs to be served, and on a practical view of the means available to achieve them. Communicating these goals clearly to the management team is vital to the success of the project, in that they provide the guidelines for action and the limitations within which the management team must work.

The strength and prestige of the sponsoring organization can do much to enhance the stature of a project. From a practical standpoint, this can be an important factor in gaining community acceptance of measures and concessions for the project that will ultimately affect the welfare of the residents. Examples of areas in which a strong sponsorship can be of use are:

Obtaining property tax abatement;

Constructing public and recreational areas and parks near the project;

Cooperating with public agencies in furnishing services and benefits for the residents;

Developing service programs and services for the residents.

These services need not be directed or provided by the management, but it is up to the management to coordinate and schedule them. Examples of such services are:

Group transportation;

Laundry and meal services;

Security and surveillance;

Leisure-time and social services.

The role of the sponsor includes supervising the overall operation of a project to insure attainment of the goals set for the property and to see that residents receive the benefits implicit in the plan. In many cases, an owner-sponsor elects to delegate the responsibility for management of the property to:

A nonprofit management board or committee;

A hired or appointed individual; or

A private management agency.

The sponsor's chairperson or other individual the sponsor designates as contact person is responsible for reporting on the project's operation. Typically, the residents in a complex form a group, hold some joint meetings with the management team, and, on occasion, elect spokespersons to summarize matters to present at a management conference. Some owner-sponsors who remain involved with the project help to cover costs of services not included in the operating expense category. This can provide resources that help make the residents' day-to-day living more meaningful, for example, through recreational trips, or through expertise such as that of a nutritionist. In addition, the board can apply the specialized knowledge of its members to specific problems, such as those requiring legal advice and accounting policy recommendations.

Sponsor-Management Planning

The initial meetings with the architects should include a CPM® or other professional property manager who has sufficient experience and background to make valuable contributions, e.g.:

Survey of needs;

Site selection;

Project size and design;

A thorough management plan.

If these factors are correctly structured, the rest of the project tends to work out satisfactorily; if not, there may well be difficulties. Concepts in the formative process can be changed; locked into poorly conceived procedures, they become difficult to remedy. Therefore, a professional property manager, e.g., a CPM®, should be assigned to determine the feasibility of the management plan.

Justification for consulting a professional property manager should be established at a preliminary planning meeting. The American Institute of Architects estimates that if the costs of constructing and operating a building were totaled over its lifetime, construction costs would represent only 3 percent and operating costs 97 percent. The management plan becomes an important measure of intent, and design must be geared for the most sensible use of the building. Poor planning means a poor building, and, ultimately, poor services to the elderly.

Survey of Needs

Demographic information should be analyzed carefully to determine the current and future retirement-age population in the area being considered. Census data should be examined to determine the rate of relocation on the part of those who have reached retirement age. Also, it is a good idea to learn the average age of those living in retirement communities nearby. Some planners have assumed that a large number of the eligible persons in the area would be prospective tenants, but it was the "old-old" who constituted the main market for it in that area. The "young-old" in that particular location preferred not to move unless their physical state or financial condition made it necessary.

A contract, or lease, answers needs on the part of the resident as well as it does the financial and other requirements of the owner and manager. The physical protection implicit in the terms answers the resident's need for security—not only physical security, but emotional security as well. It is important that the terms be drawn up in the light of a special sensitivity to the needs and propensities of the particular type of resident the project is intended to serve, recognizing, for instance, needs related to their age group, to their social or cultural backgrounds, and to the interests that make their lives productive and meaningful. An example of a bilingual contract that reflects sensitivity to the particular segment of the elderly population it serves is reproduced as Figure C.1 in Appendix C.

Site Selection

The best site for the project is a location within walking distance of shopping facilities (supermarket or convenience stores), banking facilities, religious institutions, and medical centers. This encourages a moderate and healthful amount of mobility on the part of the residents. In planning to include small shops or other conveniences in the housing complex, it is necessary to strike a careful balance with the facilities in the immediate vicinity. Sites of this type can be found in the suburbs, in semi-developed areas adjoining similar communities, and in some in-town neighborhoods. The sponsor must provide transportation to basic facilities such as the ones mentioned in this paragraph if the site chosen is not within walking distance. Industrial and commercial areas should be avoided because of the high costs of the land, environmental considerations, and also because such areas usually are deserted, to some extent, after business hours. It is most important that the site be in a safe area. For added safety, fencing or hand rails should be provided along sidewalks, particularly where the ground slopes.

Where local parking ordinances are over-restrictive, the owner should seek local zoning variances to permit residents and visitors to park in areas convenient to the dwelling units. Between 20 and 30 percent of the persons who live in housing for the elderly drive cars. In a new building, that figure might be as great as 60 percent.

Project Size and Design

Projects should be large enough to be financially feasible, but not so large that the elderly residents cannot fit themselves normally into the surrounding community. Garden apartments and high-rise buildings are especially suitable for projects such as this. A community of fewer than 50 units can be hard to manage financially; a complex of more than 350 units can be hard to manage physically. On the other hand, some exceptions not only exist, but flourish.

Pease

Outdoor sitting areas typically are used and enjoyed. Well-lighted canopy, hand rails, nonslip tiles and mats, sturdy benches in garden setting provide comfort and safety.

Design and construction decisions are shaped to some extent by local codes, land costs, local preferences, and rentals obtainable. The Architectural and Transportation Barriers Compliance Board has set minimum guidelines and requirements for accessible design that apply nationwide. All requirements must be studied carefully to see that compliance with one code, on a minimal level, does not fall short of compliance with another code that applies to that particular property. Projects should have a living plan which affords independence, freedom of movement, and protection—a plan encouraging the occupants' involvement with the interests and problems of others. Social and recreational facilities should reflect, insofar as possible, preferences of the anticipated residents. Multiple-purpose use of common areas should be encouraged; a central dining area, for instance, can be designed for off-hours use as a meeting-place or crafts workshop. Additional, perhaps adjacent space can be provided for special staff to work with individuals or small groups of residents. With the necessary emphasis on community areas, dwelling units, while adequate, need not be too large. A club-like atmosphere is desirable; where there are central dining facilities, they can, in many cases, be made an extension of the lobby area. Small, isolated lounge areas scattered throughout the building are costly to build, costly to furnish, and difficult for the management to supervise and maintain. For example, research has shown that small sitting areas away from the lobby are seldom used. Those in which management schedules activities are the ones that are used. Outdoor sitting areas typically are used and enjoyed.

A Thorough Management Plan

Under the direction of the sponsor, the development team sets up a timetable for the entire project. Each member contributes, from specialized knowledge of a different phase of the process, the information it takes to draw up a tentative work schedule, or "critical path." Funding, for example, is primarily the responsibility of the sponsor or sponsoring organization. A schedule is set up so that the individuals involved in development of the project know what funds they can count on having available to complete payment for goods and services each step of the way. In the case of a nonprofit organization, this may involve mere allocation of funds on hand, or it may involve an elaborate program of management of volunteer services to acquire the needed capital. At this point in planning, a fund earmarked for the project should exist, but a regular schedule of fund-raising may be set up to support the project on a continuing basis. Application for tax abatement and any financial assistance must be scheduled with a realistic estimate of the waiting periods and fees involved.

As many specific details as possible should be worked out, including, for example: a statement of the purpose of the project, feasibility studies, site and design considerations, preliminary plans, applications for permits, meetings with zoning boards and other groups, working drawings, the construction or conversion phase, periodic inspections of work in progress, coordination with local police/community service agencies, advertising and marketing, tenant selection and screening programs, criteria for waiting-list administration, financial management of the property as an asset, staffing, and a program for rental or sale and management of the residental units.

3 The Manager's Role

Housing—the individual's context for living—has an especially decisive effect on the lifestyle and well-being of elderly persons. Good housing provides necessary physical and social characteristics, compatible neighborhood, and supportive, conveniently accessible services. Therefore, a key management function is to understand the special problems that may affect an older resident's life, and help that person fully utilize the resources that the housing complex provides. For example, a manager who develops a buddy system renders a needed service. Buddies are neighbors who knock on each other's doors each day to check needs for aid and provide companionship. Surrogate sons and daughters also can be helpful to elderly persons who have no relatives nearby. They phone each morning to chat briefly and check on needs for the day; in addition, they run errands and provide any needed transportation. If there is no answer, they go to the apartment to see whether assistance is needed. Many members of groups sponsoring elderly housing volunteer to act as surrogates.

Well-run housing should have positive effects on the residents. The results of a survey made among the residents in one subsidized housing development provide a dramatic illustration of this point. Interviews were conducted with housing applicants who were living in physically substandard housing, or were socially isolated, or were in stressful situations, such as friction in the family. These elements are present in the lives of many persons of retirement age. In a series of follow-up interviews conducted 12 to 15 months after the move, those who had eventually moved into the complex were compared with those who had not moved from the unsatisfactory environment. Those who had not exhibited little change. Those who had moved into the complex had changed in many ways: they were happier, had more friends, were in better health, and had become more optimistic about the future. Social relationships among the movers and the other persons in their new environment had formed quickly. Some had developed into romances, and some of those had culminated in marriage. Management at all levels should keep in mind that housing for the

17

elderly can add a valuable resource to the community and make years of satisfying life possible for the retirement-age population.

The Management Team

The management team in a housing complex for the elderly constitutes an important link in the network of services for them, and, as such, should participate in the local health and welfare council, in appropriate social agencies, and in the many kinds of activities that enable the housing project to identify with and become integrated into the surrounding community. Members of the management team should find places on state, county, and local commissions on aging, and maintain close and constant touch with the programs of agencies such as the Administration on Aging and the Office of Human Development Services.

To get an idea of ideal staffing for good management of complexes of various sizes, it may be helpful to consider a few actual cases. A typical 170-unit privately-run urban senior housing complex has a staff of three: manager, assistant manager, and custodian. Two residents answer phones and take messages during managerial work breaks and on weekends, in exchange for an appreciable portion of their monthly rent. The custodian occupies a ground-floor apartment, and is on call for emergency needs during off-hours. Volunteers from the surrounding community keep regularly-scheduled hours in the complex, providing diversion, companionship, instruction in several realms of interest, occasional excursions to shopping centers and special events, and transportation for shopping. A typical public housing complex, similar in size, has a staff of comparable size, but does not employ residents; the custodian does not live on the premises. There is volunteer help from the surrounding community but not as much as is forthcoming in the neighborhood of the private facility.

A typical large nonprofit lifecare facility has grown from a capacity of 50 to nearly 500 residents. It employs an executive director full-time, with a staff of specialists in the respective medical disciplines part-time and on call, in addition to the chaplain and the full-time residential support staff. Volunteer help comes from the surrounding community and from the religious congregations sponsoring the facility.

In these examples of good management of large and lesser-size housing, one factor is pivotal: the attitude of management toward the residents. A feeling of optimism and well-being pervades the residents in facilities run by managers who welcome service to the elderly as an opportunity to exercise care and creativity to enhance the lives of these persons who are important to them. In projects where management of such facilities is regarded as "just a job," the impersonal and relatively uncaring attitude of management can be seen in staff indifference and perfunctory work, and in the withdrawal of residents from efforts at community life.

Whatever the size of the facility and the number of staff employed, there are fundamental roles to be fulfilled by management. In some well-run housing complexes, the manager wears many hats; it is the spirit and resourcefulness exhibited in day-to-day fulfillment of these roles that creates or fails to achieve success.

Management Team Selection

Selection of management team members should be based on:

Leadership and management qualities;

Ability to handle the administration of a corporation;

Knowledge of local community services and local sources of funding;

Knowledge of the aging process, mental retardation, other disabilities and handicaps, and related program elements;

Understanding and empathy with residents who are afflicted, as well as those who are willing and able to be relatively active and independent.

The Management Agent

The management agent is responsible for the day-to-day operation of the elderly housing community, for maintenance of standards, for monitoring of operational expenses, for reporting of financial status, for contracting with local agencies for programming and services, and for direct supervision of management personnel. The agent assumes the responsibilities designated within the policy guidelines of the owner/sponsor, and makes decisions on these matters, except for major program and budget changes. In areas where the sponsor lacks expertise, the agent may be called upon to set policies on the sponsor's behalf. The agent consults the sponsor before:

Action in situations not covered by written policies;

Changes in major budget items;

Major changes in program design;

Capital expenditures not included in the budget;

Decisions regarding the social, psychological or medical needs of residents.

The agent obtains all forms of insurance needed for adequate protection of the sponsor and the residents as required by law. This includes, where appropriate:

Public liability insurance;

Boiler insurance;

Fire and extended-coverage insurance;

Burglary and theft insurance;

Implied Warranty Agreements where sophisticated security systems have been installed.

In conference with the sponsor, the agent obtains a decision as to the amounts and terms of such coverage. The agent investigates all accidents or claims for damage relating to the ownership, operations, and maintenance of the housing complex, and obtains estimates of repair costs. The agent prepares full reports in writing for the sponsor, and submits them along with all the reports required by the insurance company.

The Executive Manager

Subject to the policies established by the sponsor, the executive manager sets the policies for the housing complex, and is responsible for overseeing the functions of rental agent and all staff work, including building maintenance, mobilizing the material, staff, space, and services to achieve the sponsor's goals.

The Property Supervisor

Functioning as a community worker, organizer, and developer within the housing complex for the elderly, the property supervisor enforces policy, directs staff work, monitors costs, and makes use of available resources to provide services and programs to enrich the living environment. Where resources in the neighborhood of the complex are limited or unavailable, the supervisor enlists the resident manager's help in developing group and individual activities to meet the residents' needs. These activities may include establishing a buddy system, personal visits to residents who are ill, and recreational functions such as bus trips, dances, bridge tournaments, and classes in arts and crafts. The property supervisor should know the residents well enough to assist them in difficult situations. For example, a variation in an individual's behavior might result in a misunderstanding or rejection by other residents. A wide range of problems may surface among the residents: struggling to live on a limited income and to find ways to supplement it; loneliness; feelings of inadequacy; loss of spouse; awareness of failing physical or mental health; and reluctance to accept the realities of the situation. The supervisor must be sensitive to changes in residents' needs, and able to recognize incipient problems so that timely help may be rendered. Where funds are available, it is beneficial to employ a certified social worker to handle special needs and difficulties.

The Resident Manager

As an arranger of facilities and services, the resident manager assumes a leadership role in developing community resources for a range of programs to benefit the residents, and, in addition, reach out to former and prospective residents. These programs may include: preretirement education, homemaker services, foster care for adults, nursing homes, personal or intermediate-care homes, rehabilitation services, outpatient clinics, improvement of public assistance services, and counseling on job opportunities. The degree of activity and participation in this role can range from provision of services within the elderly housing project to service on committees in the surrounding community, depending on the size of the housing complex. There should be some involvement in developing nonresident programs, in creating opportunities for older persons in the community to be of service to residents in the complex, and in creating opportunities for the complex and its residents to be of service to the community.

In housing complexes occupied by individuals whose physical and social needs vary from time to time, from person to person, and within themselves, successful managers have these attributes in common:

1. Knowledge of each resident's functional capacity, and access to listings of medical and other special counseling services that might be relevant to future needs for referral.

2. Awareness of when NOT to provide help or services in those instances when residents who can function independently stand to gain self-confidence by managing on their own.

3. The willingness and ability to search out opportunities to improve residents' capacity to live independently.

4. Consciousness that the business aspects of the management operation must be considered equal in importance to the first three traits listed.

The ability to communicate on several levels is vital to the resident manager, who seeks to draw the residents into the appropriate programs and also to present opportunities for beneficial relationships with others. It must be recognized that each of the residents is an individual, who may or may not take an interest in the community and its cultural life. Whether an interest can be stimulated or cultivated, and whether or not a particular activity is likely to benefit the individual can best be known by a resident manager who keeps in close touch with the residents, respects their individuality, and derives satisfaction from finding ways to enhance their opportunities to enjoy life.

Communication with Residents

It is important for management to recognize the differences between housing the elderly and the nonelderly. Management's realization of these differences is basic to good relationships with the residents. The majority of the residents are women in their 70s, many of whom are experiencing adverse reactions to separation from their families. They may feel that their purpose in life has diminished along with their responsibilities and involvement in the mainstream. The lines of communication should be established in a manner that leaves no doubt that what these residents think and say about the project is important to management. At the same time, tact must be exercised so that no one resident over-utilizes staff time. The following examples of devices for establishing communication lines may be of help.

Memos: Management to Residents

Information, that applies to all the residents or to a large percentage of them, can be communicated effectively through concise memos distributed to each unit's mailbox or slipped under the door of each unit. Memos on items of casual interest can simply be placed at a central distribution point, such as the central lounge, dining room, or meeting room. These memos, though brief, set the tone for day-to-day contact, and should be worded carefully to encourage the kind of management-resident relationship that is in keeping with the sponsor's goals.

Residents' Organization

Elderly persons who do not have full-time occupations have the time and experience to become excellent participants in the process of self-government. The opportunity to get together with other residents can provide the emotional support a new resident needs in order to adjust to the new environment. The organization can be meaningful to all residents as part of an ongoing socialization process. Whether activity-oriented or socially-centered, the group can promote interaction among residents and give them a medium through which to develop and practise new skills.

The most successful social programming emanates from a basic structure of democratically organized resident committees. . . . Examples of self-governing committees and clubs in elderly housing are: House & Grounds Committee, Social Program Committee, Newspaper Staff, Public Affairs Committee, Tour Committee, Welcoming Committee, Library Board, Medical Discussion Club, Volunteer Society, Gift Shop Committee, and Men's Club. Committees and clubs should meet on a regular weekly basis if at all possible. This provides the continuity necessary to carry out a well-rounded program (Joan I. Maas, CPM®, Chicago).

Residents' Committees

Committees handling complaints and other serious issues in some complexes consist totally of residents; in others, residents and representatives of management work together to find solutions to these problems. Other such committees consist entirely of management personnel. Whatever the composition of the committee, it is important that the resident be assured that management is addressing these difficulties in a manner that is fair to all.

Suggestions from Residents

Comments, suggestions and complaints are put into writing and submitted for consideration by management. This method invites candor by providing for anonymity, in case the resident should wish it. Here, too, it is important that management give serious and impartial attention to each of the items submitted.

Publications: for and by Residents

Newsletters and bulletins, whether one page issued weekly, four pages issued monthly, or some other size and frequency, reflect the kind of resident-management relationship desired by the residents, and encourage resident interaction in many ways that can be beneficial. The opportunity to express opinions, to promote events, to recognize achievements or simply the

---

M E R I V A L E   M A N O R

N E W S L E T T E R

March, 1985

HOW TO AGE GRACEFULLY--
IN 6 EASY LESSONS

Six Monday morning sessions will be devoted to study and discussion of the prospects and problems involved in the aging process. The class will meet from 10 a.m. to 11:30 a.m., starting May 6. To sign up, call Lee Gray, 932-4857

CAUTION SIGNS

PLEASE be careful when you walk through the parking lot near the bus stop. When the bus can't turn around and has to back up, the driver may not see you in the roadway.

PLEASE put out your cigarette in an ashtray even if you leave only momentarily. In that moment a blaze can flare up.

PLEASE dress as you would to go out, if you step into the hall or go to the laundry room. Nightwear belongs in the privacy of your unit.

T O   Y O U R

H E A L T H

Wednesday, March 19, at high noon, the Health and Safety Committee will host a health food lunch featuring talks by representatives of the Red Cross and the Visiting Nurses Association.

HEALTH HINTS

A healthy body is an active one. Blood health is maintained by physical movement. A daily 30-minute walk is a good way to keep your blood delivering nourishment to the organ systems needing them.

LIBRARY OFFERS
ROUND-THE-CLOCK
READY ENJOYMENT

Starting today, the library will be open on a 24-hour-basis for browsers and for those who just can't put that book down. Book reviews will be given 3 p.m. Tuesdays.

WHAT GOES ON HERE--
Events, Times, Places

The time to plant is very soon, according to Mr. Jordan, our new garden specialist. The soil is tilled, and the garden sectioned off. See him if you want to select a plot to plant and tend during the growing season.

The new nature trail is ready now. Take a short hike, or a long one, at any time of the day or evening. There's always something worthwhile to explore. Camera buffs, take plenty of film! Follow the arrows along the pathways.

Movies will be better than ever, now that Merivale and Woodhaven are pooling film funds, and seeing them together weekly. This Sunday at 7 p.m. at Woodhaven (by bus leaving promptly at 6 p.m.) we'll see "Odyssey 2010."

CHECK THE NEW
CALENDAR OF EVENTS
ON PAGE TWO!

Figure 1.
Newsletter: An Example

individuality of residents, stimulates creative efforts, and imparts the sense of belonging to a group that cares about each member. Figure 1 shows an example of a newsletter that can be produced at low cost by using a typewriter, "clip" art, and a local quick-printing service or photocopier.

Management Orientation

The responsibilities of management to residents of elderly housing in general involve a four-fold basic commitment:

1. To help individual residents maintain personal health, safety, and satisfaction with life.

2. To be aware of each resident's own goals for normal living, and, without assuming a "parent" role, encourage residents who have chronic or temporary disabilities to seek services enabling them to function on an equal basis with those who are able-bodied.

3. To provide or refer special services where they are needed and available.

4. To treat all residents as equals, and to maintain the health and safety of the community of residents as a whole.

Management and Staff Training

Training should be planned in order to upgrade the functional ability of each member of the staff. The range of opportunities for training is wide: from short (one- or two-day) sessions updating the basics or introducing new tasks to be incorporated into a job, to long-term courses equipping the employee for responsibilities at a higher level.

The Institute of Real Estate Management (IREM) in Chicago is the source of information on the training courses included in the qualifications for the CERTIFIED PROPERTY MANAGER® (CPM®) designation and the ACCREDITED RESIDENT MANAGER™ (ARM®) recognition. IREM can provide training for the various skills to be exercised in the specialized field of housing for the elderly. The National Center for Housing Management in Washington, D.C., also provides a broad range of training sessions and institutes on regional and national levels. A list of resources is included in Appendix B.

The experience of working with housing for the elderly has stimulated some managers to seek further education in gerontology or social work. On-site day-to-day management of this type of community also provides these managers with a practical viewpoint that makes such studies more vivid and useful than they might be for students who have had no immediate contact with the realities of these situations. In any case, some background in these disciplines is an invaluable asset to the management of such housing.

Service Delivery System

A workable service delivery system to fulfill the housing needs of the retirement-age population incorporates the following primary and supporting roles.

Governing Board/Managing Agent sets operating policy in conjunction with manager and assistant manager; is the final authority in all management matters, but is not to be involved in any decisions the manager can base on policy that is already established.

Manager is directly responsible to the governing board/managing agent to carry out intake and termination functions, management and property management within established operational policy; supervises the activities of any clerical and maintenance staff; hires outside contractors and consultants; with board consent, interacts with tenants' organizations; directs all on-site staff.

Assistant Manager carries out all the tasks directed by the manager; with manager's approval, works with residents' organizations.

Residents' Organization (or *Committee*) interacts directly with the manager to contribute comments and other input regarding operational policy and management practices; serves as a forum to reconcile disputes between residents; interacts with assistant manager to help coordinate aspects of social, recreational and informative programs, and staff them with volunteers.

The support staff may be large or small in number, depending on the size and level of activity in the housing complex. In the case of a small number of residents, say 50 or fewer, it is usual for the manager to assume each of these roles, including those of the supporting staff, as needed.

Basic Management Services

The basic services required to keep a housing project functioning are summarized in the following checklist.

Processing applications for residential units involves a routine check of credit references; the results, together with the prospective resident's assurance of compliance with the rules of the housing complex, complete the basis for acceptance or rejection;

Rent collection and proper crediting of payments;

Budget preparation;

Accounting and cost control;

Routine cleaning, maintenance, repair of public areas and equipment; purchase of supplies;

Development of job descriptions and schedules;

Painting and decorating of units; refurbishing of apartments between occupancies; preventive maintenance;

Repair of sponsor-owned appliances and equipment in units;

Periodic inspections of fire safety equipment and escape routes;

Tenancy termination: attempts to reconcile prior to eviction action; proper administration, and compliance with applicable laws on filing of eviction notices, or on transfer procedures.

Services to Add for the Elderly

In recognition of the needs of elderly residents for services beyond the basics listed in the foregoing passage, addition of the following should be made for management of this specialized form of housing.

Service program coordination *Security and surveillance measures* should meet the needs indicated by local conditions; they might include mechanical controls at the building entrance; an alarm system connected to the manager's office and to the nearest police and fire stations; guards at the entrance lobby; and after-hours surveillance of the property. Guard duty may be performed by qualified paid or volunteer residents who may be scheduled around the clock. Guards should be available to assist visitors and also to assist residents who have difficulty in walking or boarding vehicles.

Adaptation of units for residents with special needs should be made when the dwelling unit is refurbished between occupancies. This includes installation of conveniences such as grab bars or right- or left-handed refrigerator doors or other equipment needed by the new resident.

Counseling of residents should be aimed at resolving problems with management, such as delinquency in paying rent; or resolving problems with other tenants, such as conflicts in scheduling the borrowing of a slide projector, or of the use of a meeting-room; or consideration of a possible eviction.

Referrals to transfer housing for residents who no longer benefit sufficiently from the housing unit to remain in it should be made by the manager. This involves a search for appropriate housing, and a consultation with the resident, possibly including family members and friends, to weigh the possibilities for housing. This may also involve referral to social service agencies and to counselors in other professional disciplines.

Services not Provided by Management

In housing that integrates a population with varying degrees of health, agility, strength, and vitality—varying not only among the residents, but within each resident from month to month, and from day to day—every attempt should be made by the management to treat them all in equal fashion. Therefore, except for emergencies, the premise that an able-bodied resident should be able to act independently to secure services not supplied by the management should also hold true at times when that resident, or any other, feels in need of additional assistance in maintaining the lifestyle that has been set. Any other attitude would seriously compromise the concept of independent living.

An example of such services is the provision of part-time or full-time personnel for heavy cleaning of a unit. It should be assumed that any residents requiring these services will take steps to obtain them from community agencies, social agencies, or other public service sources in the area surrounding the housing complex. The management should be prepared to direct the resident to information concerning the availability of these services in the area.

Cooperative Planning for Services

Viewing the provision of services for residents in housing for the elderly as a community responsibility, and the morale and well-being of the retirement-age population as a community asset, the management team can work with local public agencies and private groups to add some services to those that management offers within the complex. The following guidelines can help get this cooperative work under way.

1. Establish a Planning Advisory Committee, consisting of members of the local Citizens' Council on Aging, and representatives of private and public, state and local, civic, voluntary, and profit-making health and welfare community resources, including universities. If the community has no Citizens' Council, the first step is to help form one.

2. With the committee members, review data available in the local area from the State Commission on Aging, from senior centers, and from city planning agencies, to identify the needs that exist and the resources that can be mobilized to fulfill them.

3. From committee discussions of the needs elderly persons express, and any indications of action being taken to remedy them, formulate a system of priorities for program development.

4. Establish ways to use community resources to perform these services for the elderly persons who need them, keeping in mind the priorities that have been set. Negotiate agreements with local agencies and other organizations on the nature of the services and the manner in which they are to be staffed. It is easier to secure a firm commitment when services are specified and set down in writing, with copies for all persons who are to be involved in its implementation. Delivery of services may vary as to whether a service is to be placed on-site or off the premises, whether staff members providing these services are to work full-time, part-time, or on call, and whether a multipurpose neighborhood facility might be used. For example, a local family service agency may provide a full-time counselor on-site or in a nearby senior center office; the local Social Security office may arrange for the services of a staff member twice a week to help with the details involved in submitting applications. It would be helpful if there

were a single application elderly persons might submit that would be acceptable for health, welfare, and housing services, as well as for Social Security. This application could replace the dozens of forms applicants for the various services are required to complete.

5. Draw up an Implementation Schedule, with reference to the priorities that have been set. The committee should also set up a schedule for periodic review, assessment, refinement, and further development of the program.

Staffing for Delivery of Services

The process of developing coordinated and comprehensive services for residents in housing for the elderly is the same whether the program is designed for a local housing authority involving hundreds of units or for a small, privately owned and managed multifamily development. For the larger projects, the task is best handled by a full-time professional who is skilled in community organization and has had experience in coordinating programs and services involving multiple agencies. Where there is no staff person designated as coordinator, the function should become the role of the manager, with supportive volunteer help in leadership and administration, as well as in implementation.

Professionals and paraprofessionals from the various specialized agencies and organizations in the surrounding community are the ideal volunteers to implement the community service program augmenting the resources the elderly housing complex provides. The availability of such personnel varies, with the nature of the resources in the local community. A typical community service staff for a large complex includes the following roles to be fulfilled.

1. *Program Coordinator* to implement the total delivery system, and coordinate, integrate, direct and monitor its daily operation. In a community with scattered sites, the coordinator might be responsible for the operation of several programs.

2. *Social Service Staff* to provide a wide range of counseling services for the special needs of the residents and their families, consultation to professional and volunteer staff, and training for professionals and paraprofessionals.

3. *Health Care Staff/Geriatric Specialists* to provide on-site medical services; to coordinate comprehensive health services; to train paraprofessional staff.

4. *Nutritionist/Dietitian* to coordinate a meals program.

5. *Recreational/Vocational Staff* to coordinate leisure activities to plan for and work toward occupational opportunities.

6. *Volunteer Organizer* to coordinate volunteers in delivery of services, possibly supplementing some agency services to clients. Local volunteer bureaus can be helpful in recruiting and training persons for this service. Some of the residents may wish to take the training and function as volunteers.

Managing Conflicting Needs and Interests

The scope of management services and the supplementary services offered by volunteers in the surrounding community can accommodate a variety of needs, especially in a housing complex that integrates residents who are able-bodied with those who have some degree of disability. In any combination of residents, the potential for conflict of needs and interests exists. The following areas are the ones in which this potential has been found to be the greatest.

1. *Processing of applications* It is possible for the entire intake process to be overburdened with procedures and logistics as a result of medical review and qualification requirements for applicants who have certain

disabilities. This may not only cause difficulties for the applicants, but also may cause costly delays in filling vacancies. This conflict can be eliminated by standardizing the forms and procedures for all applicants, whether able-bodied or not.

2. *Rent collection* When residents who receive varying amounts of financial assistance for housing live near those who receive none, conflicts can arise from being approached differently in the process of collecting rents. In this event, as in instance number 1, the solution lies in standardizing the procedure so that no tenant group is spotlighted by different treatment. Schedules, forms, and frequency of reminder can be set up to accommodate all variations in tenant situations within the same format, and thus give the same treatment to each one.

3. *Cleaning, maintenance, and repair* If the staff that is employed by management to perform these tasks for the public areas of the housing complex performs them within the units for tenants who are unable to do so, and if this causes any neglect of public areas, some tenants may raise objections. Some complexes provide basic cleaning services for unit interiors; others do not. In complexes that do not provide unit interior cleaning services, tenants are responsible for hiring any needed cleaning services from an outside source. Management should be prepared to provide a list of reasonably-priced sources for these services.

4. *Service program coordination* Conflicts can arise when the time spent in coordinating service programs appears to usurp the administration of the basic management services. To avoid these conflicts, and to encourage independence on the part of the residents, responsibility for coordinating the programs of service from the community surrounding the complex can be placed in the hands of a volunteer—or, better still, a volunteer organization.

5. *Resident groups with differing interests* The "young-old" may see the "old-old" as receiving more management time and consideration, curtailing services to residents in general, or the "old-old" may see the "young-old" as using more than their share of the public spaces for meetings or events benefitting only a portion of the residents. Some residents who are able-bodied may not wish to have their rental money support special conveniences for the exclusive use of disabled persons. To minimize conflict, management personnel should handle services provided equally for all residents, and leave the administration of services with limited participation to other staff or to volunteer organizations.

Minimizing Conflict Potential

Structure of the management service delivery system can incorporate elements that minimize or avert potential conflicts. Whether the residents of the complex are disparate or relatively homogeneous in their needs and interests, and whether most are able-bodied or disabled, experience in coping with the needs and problems of the disabled is essential. For example, a workable combination of backgrounds for management of units integrating able-bodied and disabled residents would be a manager with a background in business and property management, assisted by a person experienced in dealing with the disabled.

Manager: At Home On-Site

Problems of safety, health, resident relations, and community activity can require immediate attention on the part of management at any time of the day or night. For this reason, it is desirable for some member of the management staff to live in one of the units of the housing complex. It is not always possible for the executive manager to do so, but solutions can be worked out such as having one of the following live on the premises:

The manager or assistant manager;

A custodial family;

A responsible student;

A homemaker or caretaker—

OR—A resident who is willing and able to assume the responsibility to take the appropriate action in case of emergency.

Management Planning

A basic difference between the management of housing in general and housing for the elderly in particular is the importance of the passage of time and the changes that result. Few persons go abruptly from a state of independence to a need for help with the routine tasks of living. In many there is a lengthy period of diminishing physical vigor that must be taken into account in planning the use of resources months and years ahead. The successful manager places social and physical management on an equal basis with business management in looking to future needs and opportunities.

4   Managing the Housing Process

Fundamental to the housing process are the policies formulated by the sponsor, before or during the planning sessions with the manager, to establish the type of housing being sponsored, the qualifications for admission of applicants, and the conditions governing retention and termination of residential privileges. Before adopting any policy regarding requirements and conditions for admission or retention, it is vital to have the specific wording reviewed by legal counsel to see that it contains no possible conflict with local or national codes or statutes, and also to see that the provisions of the policy are practicable, enforceable, and in keeping with the goals that have been set for the housing project. Policies should be reviewed regularly to see whether any changes in legislation or other factors indicate that amendments should be considered.

Housing Policies

The review of applications for acceptance in a housing unit is an example of an area where policy must be set. The final authority for acceptance of an applicant in some projects is the manager, in others it is the board of directors. The procedure becomes more complicated in housing that accommodates residents with permanent disabilities, and still more complicated when the project incorporates a health care facility. In the latter case, policy is dictated to a great extent by certification and licensing requirements. The project's policies should also reflect management's concern with liability and responsibility for tenants and their property. For instance, in case of fire, it is vital to know whether all residents are ambulatory and whether they can all be expected to follow the procedures outlined for emergency action. Written statements of policy should be used by staff members, the managerial team, the sponsor, the board of directors, and any volunteer organizations providing assistance, to provide a proper perspective for decision-making and action. Careful adherence to a set of well-formulated policies can simplify the manager's work; at the same time, it assures residents that they can depend on the services and conditions to which these policy statements refer. The HUD form excerpt in Appendix C (Figure C.3) is an example of a statement of admissions policy that is in use throughout a wide-ranging, complex housing system. The following is another example of a policy statement.

You may stay as long as you do not endanger the life and safety of others; you must submit a physician's statement that you are in good health and able to take care of yourself, that you do not have a drug-abuse or drinking problem or need assistance to take medication; you must be able to go downstairs on your own in case of fire; you must be able to live independently and maintain your own household without asking help or depending on our staff or your neighbors.

In addition to stated formal and informal policies, the project's on-site staff, the management firm, housing authority staff, and, in most cases the board of directors, should have a general understanding as to what circumstances would call for reconsidering the continuing occupancy of a unit by the resident in question. Some of these policies may require flexibility in dealing with specific tenants or they may involve the sensitive issue of mental competence and emotional stability, and therefore may be difficult to spell out in a written policy statement, but they are no less important than the other policies for the staff and applicant to understand and accept.

Consistency in making and following policies, and in scheduling policy reviews, are important factors in working toward trouble-free management. For example, it has been found that, in general, there is not much consistency between admission and retention policies of the various types of housing for the elderly. In a large number of these projects, some problems acceptable in applicants are found to be unacceptable if residents develop them. What has happened, in many cases, is that admissions policies have been altered as management has gradually changed its views of what constitutes independence in living, but there have been no corresponding retention policy changes. There appears to be a general acceptance of changes in eyesight, hearing, mobility, and basic health. Retention is most often called into question when severe problems develop; e.g., overmedication and alcohol abuse, reclusive behavior, and symptoms attributed to senility or accident-proneness, requiring daily supervision or skilled nursing care.

Preoccupancy Planning

Plans basic to occupancy are made initially by the sponsor and manager, often in conjunction with representatives of government assistance programs. It is when inquiries are made by persons seeking elderly housing that the efficacy of those plans begins to be tested. If accurate figures and facts have resulted from the indications of nationwide and local demographic trends, from the estimates of the nature and extent of the housing needed by the respective retirement-age levels, and from figures on income levels of these age groups, then housing for those who wish it will be available and affordable in the locations they prefer. If not, immediate needs can be satisfied only through compromise, and housing managers have a mission to accomplish in bringing the real and ongoing needs of the elderly to the attention of planners, government agencies, and the general public.

In the initial interview with the inquirer or applicant, the manager presents and explains the project's admissions policy. This is also an opportunity for the manager to make a preliminary judgment regarding the type of housing situation most appropriate for that individual's current, near-future, and long-term needs. If there is an indication that the applicant may not be able to live independently, and that another type of housing might better answer the needs that are evident, the person can be referred directly to it. For instance, a person who can be relatively, but not totally independent, might be referred directly to a source of congregate housing and be spared the discomfort of striving for a level of independence that is unrealistic. On the other hand, the same level of disability in an "independent living" situation might present a workable challenge to a person sufficiently motivated to initiate self-help, and when needed, to procure needed assistance. A visit to the applicant at home can provide the manager with the background needed to make the decision.

Norms of Living Capabilities

Establishing some norms of living capabilities appropriate to the type of housing that the project provides for the elderly enables the management to maintain safe and decent housing conditions for a population whose needs in this context, in general, can be predicted. These norms for the project also make it possible to make the most effective and efficient use of the social, health, and financial resources available. Guidelines have been developed to gauge routine living skills and habits. A 20-item example of two kinds of factors—critical and contributory—is reproduced in Appendix C. "Critical factors" relate directly to lease requirements or to immediate health and safety conditions. "Contributory factors" relate to them indirectly. The critical and contributory factors affecting a person's ability to live independently are weighed to determine which of the three basic categories is most appropriate.

1. Independent living.
2. Semi-independent living.
3. Supported living.

These norms form a continuum upon which the status of an individual resident's condition can be charted and defined. To ensure objectivity, they should be used within the context of case conferences involving all personnel working with a resident. The resident should be encouraged to participate in the decision-making process, and should be given any support needed. Decisions should be made by team consensus. For example, assume that a particular resident is functioning within the second category. Over time, the social services team members can use the norms to determine whether the individual is moving toward the first or third category. An assessment of the individual's status over this time period provides the case team with a chance to work realistically and sensitively toward a satisfactory case plan and development.

Even if an evaluation over a period of time indicates that the resident is moving toward the third category, this does not necessarily mean that the resident needs to live in a highly structured setting staffed by health care professionals—that is, a need for residential, intermediate, or skilled nursing care—but it does mean that the living environment—either the project itself or the neighborhood surrounding it—should constitute a source of the services needed by the resident. If a resident's skill level in ten or more of the 20 skills or habits evaluated falls within the second category, the management team should consider the possibility of an alternative living situation and lay some groundwork with the resident and any concerned family members regarding possible placement elsewhere.

Intake Procedures

The manager or assistant manager interviews the applicant and shows the apartment or other dwelling unit, explaining available services, management attitudes, expectations of residents, and criteria for acceptance. The application form, designed carefully to fit the requirements for that specific type of housing, is filled out at this meeting or given to the applicant to mail in. An example of an application form that reflects careful planning is reproduced here.

Upon receipt of the completed application form, the manager and clerical staff check on the details of income level. If the applicant has a problem qualifying for this type of housing and the manager is responsible for a decision on the basis of policy and the guidelines that exist, but cannot decide, the application may be referred to the property supervisor. When the process is completed, the manager and clerical staff convey the acceptance, waiting-list status, or rejection to the applicant. On acceptance, if any special adaptations are needed, the manager schedules the maintenance staff to install them.

Resident's Orientation

A significant factor distinguishing the professional property manager from the novice is management technique. As it specifically applies to the process of moving into an elderly housing facility, the proper technique can be useful in reducing the potential for problems and dissatisfactions the resident might experience in the future. Some management techniques are described in the following paragraphs.

Resident's Handbook

Good management technique is exemplified by the production of a handbook for residents that clearly and succinctly spells out house rules and the resources, restrictions, and emergency directions relating to the occupancy of the unit. Diagrams and written directions should identify and show the location of the major features of the housing complex, such as the business office, laundry facilities, lounge, snack bar, craft and television rooms, and emergency evacuation routes. Instructions for operating appliances, service request procedures, rent collection procedures, and late charge schedules should be included. Outside resources serving project residents should be identified and mapped in like manner. Examples are: the nearest public transportation, bus stop, grocery store, drug stores, doctor's office, church and synagogue, senior citizens' center, library, post office, and movie theatres. The Handbook should be available for consultation upon inquiry or application, and given to the prospective resident upon the signing of the lease or contract. The following paragraphs describe some of the subjects to be covered in the Handbook.

Guided Tour of the Premises

Using the map and diagram in the Handbook, the manager or assistant manager should take the new resident on a guided tour of the premises, pointing out the best routes to take to the major features, and the schedules for events and facilities, adding any other information the Handbook may or may not contain. The tour affords the resident an opportunity to ask questions, and jot the answers down in the Handbook as a reference. In a multistory building, it is important to show the resident how to locate and operate any self-service elevators.

Visits to the Unit

The Handbook should explain that the maintenance superintendent and staff make periodic visits to each unit to check on needs for maintenance and repair of the equipment. An initial visit on moving into the unit should provide instruction and practice in operating the kitchen equipment, the emergency call system, and any special devices installed to enable a disabled resident to be

Health Care

Each resident is responsible for the cost of any medical care.

Every resident must have an annual physical examination by a licensed physician. Please have the doctor fill out the special medical examination form for the files.

Every resident must have regular bi-annual dental check-ups.

Every resident should have eye examinations at least every two years, more often if necessary.

Conservation

Pleasant View Home, Inc., has tried very hard to build a facility which is energy-efficient and comfortable. Please try to help keep costs down and be a wise consumer of energy by following these tips:

1. Turn off lights, radios, televisions, etc., when not in use.
2. Thermostats should remain constant at an energy-saving level.
3. When using appliances such as washers, dryers, dishwashers, etc., use when *full*, but not overcrowded.
4. Use warm or cold water when hot water is not necessary. Do not leave water running when not in use.
5. Outside windows or doors should not be kept open longer than necessary while heating or air conditioning units are in operation.

Care of Grounds

To help make your home more attractive to you, your guests, and the community, landscaping and lawn care are carefully maintained.

All of you will be given an opportunity to help with the yard work according to your interests and abilities (e.g., cutting grass, pulling weeds, caring for flowers, raking leaves, etc.). Maintenance personnel will assist in the lawn and landscaping care.

You are encouraged to plant an annual vegetable garden which will give you nutritious fresh foods. There are many jobs in the garden which you can be a part of: planting seeds, weeding, watering, harvesting, or preparing foods for the freezer.

Apartment Care and Usage

This is your home. We want it to be a pleasant, comfortable, clean and safe place to live. Each of you will be encouraged to share responsibilities in maintaining areas other than your own unit. Remember to always clean up after your activities in public areas so that someone else will not have to.

Den

This is a TV and game room to be used for group or individual leisure time. Try to be considerate of others when using items in this room by keeping the noise level down and by returning used items to their proper places.

Living Room

This is to be used as a reception and visiting area for your guests.

Kitchen, Dining Area and Pantry

Because of health standards, all food service areas should be kept as clean and sanitary as possible. Please wash your hands before eating or working in food preparation. Foods should be properly stored to avoid attraction of insects or rodents. You will be encouraged to limit food and drink items to the kitchen, dining area, and your own unit.

Guest Bathroom

This is the guest bathroom and can also be used as a utility bathroom when working in the kitchen.

Laundry Room

There will be two pay washers and two pay dryers for your use. The fee for each load is comparable to that of a self-service laundry. You will be responsible for your own weekly laundry and you will need to buy your own laundry detergent. When using the dryer, always remember to clean the lint cage. The laundry area should be left clean for the next person to use, and should be cleaned weekly.

An Outside Dumpster

This dumpster is provided for trash which includes paper products, glass, cans, etc. Most food wastes (except bones) may be put into the kitchen garbage disposal.

Figure 2.
Resident's Handbook:
Excerpts

independent. A followup visit several days later should be useful in checking on any difficulty the resident might have considered too minor to warrant a call for help. These periodic visits also enable the staff to check on any changes in the resident's health, financial, or social needs that might alert the management to a need for further services or other accommodations.

Buddy System

For the mutual benefit of the residents, the Handbook should explain, the Buddy System provides that each resident check daily to see that an assigned neighbor is all right, and, if not, follows emergency instructions to summon help. Buddies alert each other to planned absences and visitors, and help their new neighbors get acquainted with other residents.

Project/Community Activity

The Handbook should invite the new resident to participate in whatever activities exist within the complex and in the surrounding community, giving details such as general schedules and names and telephone numbers of the persons coordinating the events. The particulars that are subject to frequent change, such as meeting dates, hours, or locations, can be set forth on separate sheets, to be photocopied or quick-printed, and placed in mailboxes, or in a central location for pickup. A calendar mounted on a bulletin board can help coordinate schedules and remind residents of events to come. The deadline for information to be included in the next newsletter can be included. The bulletin board can function as a message board for residents to use in contacting each other, thereby relieving the switchboard and office staff of the burden of inquiries when changes are made in scheduled events; it can also be used as a medium of communication between management and residents.

A calendar mounted on a bulletin board can help coordinate schedules, reminding residents and management of newsletter deadlines and events to come.

HUD

Termination of Residence: Death

If the sole occupant of a dwelling-unit dies alone in the unit, the police department should be notified immediately; the names and phone numbers of the next of kin, or friends, should be available to them when they arrive. The lock on the door should be changed at once. The manager does not act as the executor of an estate or hold any funds in escrow or in safekeeping for residents. All funds, accounts, and personal property of the deceased resident have been the resident's responsibility to hold or assign. If a relative or friend carrying proper identification requests entry, accompany the person into the unit. Do not allow removal of papers or other items without authorization. Request that the relative handling the estate (belongings) of the deceased obtain "Letters of Administration" from the local estate court. This document names the individual(s) who are responsible for handling the affairs of the deceased. The cost is low (usually $10.00 for estates under $5,000.00). Any other documents, such as power of attorney, become void upon the death of the individual named in them. The family member who initially enters the dwelling unit should sign a release stating that he or she is indeed the next of kin, and will hold the property owner and staff harmless against any suit from any relative for items removed by the person signing the release. The manager should work with the family if additional time is needed beyond the term of paid rental to complete handling of the affairs of the deceased.

Termination of Residence: Voluntary

In a termination initiated by the resident, the manager or assistant manager should attempt reconcilement through an in-depth interview exploring the reasons for the contemplated departure. There are times when a breakdown in communication results in a hasty decision by the resident, who may have no idea that the management might have the resources to come up with a satisfactory solution or alternative that would make continued residence not only feasible, but desirable. This interview may also bring out a need for improvement of services, or for conferences with another resident or residents, or for outside services the manager can arrange or recommend.

Whatever the outcome, it is important to document these interviews and keep them on file. In addition to functioning as supporting evidence for decisions on the case at hand, this file becomes valuable as a basis for future consideration of changes in acceptance and other policies. If the result in the case at hand is termination, the manager or assistant manager handles the paperwork and logistics of moving, and may also be needed by the resident to involve outside agencies in the search for other housing. The procedure for final billing and collection of rent and other fees involved is the same for all residents, whether the termination of residence is voluntary or involuntary.

Termination of Residence: Involuntary

In termination decisions based on problems such as social incompatibility, it is the manager's responsibility to make serious attempts at reconcilement, giving each person involved a fair chance to contribute to the resolution of the case. As in voluntary termination decisions, there is, in many cases, a good chance that the problems or differences can be worked out to the satisfaction of all without a change in residence. If that does not appear to be possible, the manager follows whatever policy has been set for the housing complex. Some policies require a hearing with the property supervisor. If the decision is termination, the manager must give the resident due notice of eviction, and follow the eviction procedure that has been set, in accordance with local laws and any federal restrictions that apply. If the termination decision is based on a disability the housing complex cannot accommodate, or an increase in disability to a point making continued residence infeasible, the decision may be referred to a medical board. The manager bases the termination on the board's opinion, and proceeds as with voluntary termination. The manager may need to seek the help of outside agencies to find transfer housing that meets the needs of the individual.

5 Managing Independent Living

Statistics on the characteristics of residents in housing for the elderly who are able to live independently indicate that the majority of residents are women in their late 70s and who have to cope with some physical, social and financial problems. With some initial assistance in gaining access to the information and resources they need, they can manage on their own. The manager's patience, time, and care are needed to help make this transition to the new environment. For many of these residents, the necessity to adjust to new living quarters is concurrent with the pain of adjusting to the loss of a spouse or other family member, and of parting with good neighbors and familiar surroundings. The sense of loss is accompanied by some uncertainty about what the future will hold. About 50 percent of the persons who move into housing for the elderly for the first time have been homeowners; they face a drastic change in their lifestyle. The manager can ease the way for the resident's transition to a new life that holds promise for the future.

Knowing the Resident

In no other type of housing is it more important for the manager to appreciate the individuality of each resident, and, in a very real sense, to know that person. This is particularly true because of the tendency of the general public to ignore individuality in the elderly. Reacting to the elderly as a group marked by diminished capabilities and value to society becomes a self-fulfilling prophecy when it lowers morale and limits opportunities. Such reactions result from the popularization of false generalizations about the characteristics of this age group.

We must reconceptualize the roles of older people in our society. No longer should the vast majority be perceived solely as dependents, but rather as valued individuals, most of whom can function well in society, albeit with an increased risk for specific problems (Carl Eisdorfer, "Conceptual Models of Aging," *American Psychologist* [February 1983], p. 197).

Knowing the Elderly Population

The facts about the elderly population as tenants in apartment buildings are spelled out in a widely-used text:

Senior citizens, married or not, who are secured by retirement benefits, also are a favorite tenant type. Characteristics of this group are that they tend to be quiet, prompt in paying rent, and have good housekeeping habits. Such people also tend to choose small apartments, especially when they are constrained by fixed, inflation-eroded incomes. Budgetary limitations may keep senior citizens from living in preferred neighborhoods; still, they will be discriminating in finding a place where basic daily needs can be met. It is true that the medical problems associated with advanced age may present some management problems. But beyond that, senior citizens form a most desirable segment of the market (Edward N. Kelley, cpm® and cre [Counselor of Real Estate], *Practical Apartment Management*, Second Edition [Chicago: Institute of Real Estate Management, 1981], p. 31).

Commonly-accepted myths about aging are listed here, with summaries of the relevant realities:

1. Growing old comes by getting older. (Fact: The lengthy period of extreme frailty and vulnerability associated by most persons with old age actually happens in only a small percentage of those in the retirement years.)

2. It would be better to be younger than you are. (Fact: Attitudes prejudicial toward the elderly create this impression.)

3. Intelligence declines with age. (Fact: Tests of intelligence and learning capacity have proven that the functioning of the mind not only does not decline with age, but can continue to grow.)

4. Forgetting is a sign of senility. (Fact: The need to become better listeners, common to people of all ages, causes forgetting. Forgetting by elderly persons is labeled senility by those who lack understanding of the term.)

5. Losing brain cells diminishes thinking power. (Fact: The brain loses cells every day and may even diminish in size, but the amount of loss is not only negligible—it is unrelated to thinking power.)

6. To age is to become senile. (Fact: Isolation, depression, poor nutrition, drug abuse, and infections are among more than a hundred correctable conditions that cause symptoms labeled by the uninformed as senile dementia.)

"Senility is not an inevitable consequence of growing old; in fact, it is not even a disease. . . . Rather, 'senility' is a word used to describe a large

---

One persistent bit of folklore about the brain is that we lose a vast number of brain cells as we grow old and senility is often associated with the shrinkage of brain tissue and the loss of brain cells; many people assume that mental and physical deterioration are the inevitable companions of aging. As a neuroanatomist I have been intrigued by this myth of the disappearing brain cells especially because the fact "has a sinister side." It lends a spurious air of scientific validity to our practice of relegating old people to empty, meaningless lives. When I search the scientific literature I fail to find a single thorough study which showed changes in the brain cell counts of mammals as they age. Conversely, it seems clear that inactivity is as detrimental to the brain capacity of people as it is to that of rats. The worst thing we can do is to consign elderly people to sedentary confinement in an unstimulating nursing home. To do so is to perpetuate the fallacy that brain cell loss and mental deterioration inevitably accompany old age (Marion C. Diamond, professor of anatomy, University of California, Berkeley, "Aging and Cell Loss: Calling for an Honest Count," *Psychology Today,* [September 1976], p. 126).

Symptoms of "senility" are not confined to the retirement-age population. Dr. Frances Carp of Wright Institute, Berkeley, California, reported finding more "senile" characteristics in test results of college sophomores than in those of elderly persons.

number of conditions with an equally large number of causes, many of which respond to prompt and effective treatment." (Special Report on Aging—National Institutes of Health, 1979).

7. An "old dog" can't learn new tricks. (Fact: Elderly persons have the capacity to learn virtually anything they think worthwhile.) (Tilman R. Smith, *In Favor of Growing Older* [Scottdale, Pa.: Herald Press, 1981], p. 17.)

Government-Assisted Housing Residents

Concepts of independent living in private-sector complexes, whether nonprofit or for-profit, have broadened over the past several decades, through the learning experiences managers of elderly housing have had in coping with changes in the health and living habits of residents. In general, managers accept changes in eyesight, hearing, mobility, and minor health matters in elderly residents as they accept them in the younger segments of the population. By the same token, the changes that commonly suggest alternate living arrangements are the same for elderly housing as they are in housing for younger persons: alcoholism and overmedication, reclusive or deviant behavior, and accident-proneness.

To fully understand the restrictions placed on admissions into government-assisted housing, it may be helpful to trace some aspects of the history of housing assistance. As mentioned in an earlier chapter, the first homes for the aged made no distinction among the motivants for application. Those who were in good health but lacked the funds to support separate households were welcomed under the same roof with persons who suffered from illnesses or chronic disabilities. Residents and their families paid what they could afford. Donations from congregations, individuals, and businesses supplemented these funds. Residents were sent to hospitals when the need arose, and returned to the home upon recovery. There were no provisions for assistance from the government, no tax money was available, and there were no laws regulating the operation of these homes. The persons and organizations operating and sponsoring these homes did not consider themselves part of an industry because they functioned on a nonprofit basis. It was not until the infusion of tax money motivated profit-oriented persons to enter this field, and until they organized groups to influence legislators to obtain more tax dollars, that the nonprofit homes formed their own organizations, such as the National Council on the Aging. Their work resulted in the formation of the American Association of Homes for the Aging. But some significant decisions had been made by the legislators before the administrators of the nonprofit homes could summon sufficient organizational strength to exert an influence.

One of the most far-reaching of these decisions was the separation of living quarters for the elderly from facilities incorporating health care. The Federal Housing Administration (FHA), in 1954, developed the FHA-231 program, enabling nonprofit sponsors to finance retirement homes through federally-insured mortgages. Admissions to these homes were restricted to healthy persons 62 or more years of age; no health care could be provided on the premises. To use this plan, managers of elderly housing would have to ignore what they had observed: that most persons preferred to remain in their own homes or rental apartments unless an illness or chronic disability made it necessary to move into housing that provided supportive services; also, that health varies among the elderly from day to day and week to week just as it does in the general populace. No one can guarantee to retain 100 percent good health every day of the year. The FHA administrators came to realize this after the program had been in operation for some time, and buildings had been erected that had doorways too narrow for wheelchairs, and kitchens, bathrooms and halls that lacked grab-and-grip devices. They authorized the addition of an infirmary to such buildings, with the following restrictions: one bed for each dozen residents, to be balanced by one unoccupied bed in the residential section of the complex. Because this constituted health care, even on a limited basis, the Department of Health, Education and Welfare (HEW) required that each state health department license each of these complexes— difficult because they had not been constructed with HEW requirements as guidelines. These programs serving the same population—HEW, focusing on human needs, and HUD, focusing on housing finance—at times overlapped and conflicted. A new program was developed—FHA 232—for elderly persons requiring health care, but, because this, too, segregated persons according to the state of their health, it did not fulfill the need for a flexible type of housing that could accommodate fluctuating needs for health care. Most small communities could support only one nonprofit elderly housing project, and that one would be expected to accommodate the total spectrum of needs, residential and health-related, in the local retirement-age population.

Factors in Independent Living

What constitutes independent living, then, is spelled out by government regulations, but, in practice, can vary according to the discretion of the manager and the policies of the sponsor. Compassionate managers, reluctant to transfer residents of many years' standing and increased needs for support services, have exercised ingenuity in seeking aids such as volunteer services within the community. There is a continual need to review policies for admission and retention with regard to the following three factors.

1. The range of tenant problems acceptable in residents and applicants.
2. Problems or changes viewed by the on-site staff as needs for additional assistance.
3. The role of design factors, on-site service, HUD project sponsorship, age of tenants in the project, and the experiences of management and on-site staff in influencing policy, attitude, and practice regarding the residency of persons whose capabilities have changed.

Resident Activities

The quality of activities and services the project employs can make a tremendous difference in the resident's morale and state of health, and can increase the length of time that that resident can be comfortably retained within the project. The process of developing coordinated and comprehensive services for residents is the same whether the program designed is for a local housing authority with hundreds of units or for a small, privately owned and managed multifamily development. This means employing a full-time professional skilled in community organization, with experience in coordinating programs and services of multiple agencies, or, in a small project, the manager plus volunteers.

A typical home for the aged in the nineteenth century and early in this century, though lacking in the technology and medical resources available today, did excel in creating a close-knit group of residents who played an active role in maintenance of their communal household.

A good amount of physical and occupational therapy was practiced, although no one called it that. Without a name or label, reality orientation was a normal procedure. No colored signs proclaimed, "Today is Tuesday"—

HUD

Elderly persons, like the rest of the population, need purposeful activity.

residents knew yesterday was Monday because clothes were washed and today was Tuesday because clothes were ironed and put away! Residents washed and dried dishes, cleared tables, swept floors and did other meaningful and helpful chores. The men helped the custodian, worked in the gardens, and assisted in whatever way they could. No one had to do these things. They wanted to do them—and in this way they helped themselves as well as the home (John M. Mason, *The Fourth Generation* [Minneapolis, Minn.: Augsburg Publishing House, 1978], p. 163).

There is no joy to be had from retirement except by some kind of productive work. Otherwise, you degenerate into talking to everybody about your pains and pills and income tax. Any oldster who keeps at even part-time work has something worthwhile talking about. He has a zest for the morning paper and his three meals a day. The point of all this is not to retire from work or you will shrivel up into a nuisance to all mankind (Herbert Hoover).

I am not going to make any more hot pot holders. I have made enough for a lifetime (Grace G., resident in retirement complex).

Resident Involvement

Involvement of residents with each other and with the life of the community surrounding the complex is a hallmark of success in managing housing for the elderly. Enrichment of the environment can be accomplished only to the extent that it is relevant to the residents' potential interests and abilities. To be involved in activity that is meaningful, not only in terms of the resident's interests and abilities, but also in terms of meaning and service to others, is the crucial factor for a life of invigorating challenge, kindling enthusiasm for the future. Elderly persons, like the rest of the population, need purposeful activity—whether it is paid or volunteer work, or an absorbing hobby. They need to balance it with social interaction and rest, and they wish to regulate their own schedules to the fullest extent possible.

Involvement can begin with the buddy system and radiate outward as the resident becomes acquainted with others, explores the complex's resources, and learns of upcoming events. Initial efforts to welcome a new resident should continue until the manager sees that the person is comfortably established in a satisfying way of life.

Adult Education/ Workshops

Senior centers in the community and separate facilities within housing complexes have been popular locations for the formation of workshops teaching skills such as handicrafts for women and woodworking for men. The addition of teachers—volunteer or paid—from other fields of endeavor, and access to additional materials, books, and equipment have greatly expanded the spectrum of choices, and persons such as Grace G., quoted in a foregoing paragraph, need no longer become weary of "busy" work. This can be an opportunity to retrain for a retirement-years career. An important addition is the access, in many communities, to instruction in the technology of what, according to the specialists, will constitute the "cottage industries" of the future, wherein the worker who is confined to the home will have an opportunity to participate in the mainstream of the labor force. This can constitute a solution to some of the financial and social problems now experienced during the advancing years.

Currently, the most popular subjects are budgeting, nutrition, sewing, and English. These courses are offered by public schools, large businesses and industries, health and welfare agencies, private voluntary agencies, local colleges, universities, and business schools. Many waive or reduce tuition fees for retirement-age students, and some provide courses designed to answer needs for information on issues, problems or changes in legislation relating to the retirement years.

Libraries

If a room with shelves and seating is available, a permanent library can be organized. The library can be more than a source of reading material; it can also be a meeting-place where persons may share common interests. Residents can donate books and take turns serving as librarian; if desired, the library can be open on a 24-hour-a-day basis. Books and magazines are printed in large type for the benefit of those who have visual impairments. Volunteers can read to those whose vision is more limited and to residents with literacy limitations. If there isn't a bookmobile (mobile library service) in the community, a volunteer can pick up books from the local library and deliver them to residents on request. A service such as this can become the most widespread form of adult education and recreation throughout the housing complex because of its flexibility with regard to variety of subject matter, numbers of persons served and hours of service.

Skills Exchange

Residents who are specialists (retired teachers, musicians, technicians, and hobbyists, for example) can organize and conduct workshops, study groups, discussion sessions and presentations of crafts, artwork and music. Sharing and enhancing their skills, knowledge, and interests can contribute to feelings of self-worth and enjoyment of camaraderie in their mutual endeavors.

Counseling

Planning for counseling services requires sensitivity on the part of the manager, first in recognizing these needs, if counseling is not requested, and, second, in setting up a situation conducive to effective outreach. For example, it is advantageous to arrange for counseling services to be given in surroundings that are private, and removed from earshot of places such as a recreation room or business office. Whether the need for counseling relates to Social Security information, employment, volunteer service opportunities, health insurance, legal advice, availability of welfare funds, or spiritual guidance, the manager must see that it is administered by a competent advisor in a setting conducive to confidentiality. There are times when the need for counseling can be answered by a fellow resident who is knowledgeable and can keep the matter confidential if need be. It is up to the manager, if the resident in need does not take the initiative, to recognize the need and find the most helpful way to a solution.

Recreation/Events

Patience and continued efforts can draw the shyest residents into groups celebrating holidays and birthdays, into citizenship projects, and into political activity, on a communitywide or residencewide level. Voting is a right that many elderly persons find difficult to exercise because they lack information about the candidates and issues, because they are too dispirited to believe that their vote is significant, or because they need physical assistance to reach the polling place and do not believe that they are in a position to request it. Some complexes establish the premises as a polling place for the convenience of residents, and, throughout the year, hold public-interest forums, inviting local legislators to speak. There should be a regular schedule of events, but time should be left open for residents to initiate and conduct events relating to their own special interests.

The Clergy

Local members of the clergy constitute an important link with the project management in providing residents with continuity in worship and opportunities for fellowship with others of the same faith. They also constitute a prime source of referrals for counseling residents who have questions or problems. Members of the clergy should be invited to contact new residents, and the management may wish to invite the clergy to attend any special events or celebrations that are held on the premises of the housing complex.

Friendly Visitors

Especially for residents who have no relatives or friends in the vicinity of the complex, it is important to see that there is contact with persons from the surrounding community. The citizen who volunteers to knock on a resident's door from time to time and sit down for a friendly chat can lift the morale of a person who might not venture out to initiate contact. A patient and cautious approach can break down the barriers of shyness that may exist, and the visitor may, in the course of a conversation, find that there are unmet needs that management can remedy, if informed about them.

Homemakers/Home Health Aides

Help with household chores such as cleaning, cooking, and light laundry, and with minor health services such as keeping medication and personal care on schedule, even for just a few hours a day or week, can keep many residents in an independent living situation indefinitely. These helpers are neither maids nor nurses, and there is no national licensing program for them; they simply constitute a helping hand in time of need—which may be permanent or temporary, such as the case of someone just released from the hospital in the expectation of full or partial recovery from an illness or accident. From a listing of just 300 such services in 1963, the number of agencies that are sources of this kind of help has grown to more than 5,000, throughout the United States. About half of these are certified for Medicare. Some are licensed or certified by the state. Many are approved by the National Home Caring Council, which publishes a yearly directory. It is estimated that there are about 100,000 of these helpers; because the demand for them is about three times that figure, many communities have set up training courses to increase the number available locally.

Mobility and Transportation

Specialized buses, many with special safety features, are provided in some areas to convey the elderly in these complexes to frequently-visited destinations.

Local transit companies arrange reduced fare systems for buses, and, in some areas, for taxis. For example, Dial-a-Ride, in some places, provides $1.00 rides to health appointments. Fare reductions of 50 percent or more have been arranged by civic organizations reimbursing the transit companies. Usually, fare reductions are not available during rush hours; hours of availability are announced in advance. The manager should be sure the wording of such announcements is clear to all who are interested; e.g., whether it will be a trip-by-trip discount, or the purchase of a pass good for a limited time period. Some local agencies provide a driver for residents of elderly housing complexes, at no charge, five days a week, or on an appointment basis. Specialized buses with special routes are provided in some areas to convey the elderly in these complexes to frequently-visited destinations, such as the health center, Social Security office, welfare agencies, and the post office. Some operate on a fare basis, some free of charge. Many of these buses are designed with special safety features such as ramps, or fewer steps, for the convenience of persons who find boarding the bus a slow and laborious chore. Because

HUD

passengers on these buses understand the difficulties some of them experience, they value the driver's patience and safety considerations beyond the merits of keeping firmly to a schedule. Whether cars, minibuses, or specially-designed vehicles are used, the driver's sensitivity to the passengers' needs, as shown in helping passengers to get on or off the vehicle, and to handle passengers with packages, is essential to their safe passage and enjoyment of the trip.

Multilingual/Ethnic Groups

Residents of a tightly-knit ethnic group or community dominated by one nationality to whom English may be a second language have special needs to be served by the elderly housing complex to which they move. They need to be in the mainstream of activity, and they also must be able to follow their accustomed way of life as closely as possible, including the festivals and religious observances it encompasses. This is an opportunity for residents to get to know a variety of cultures and customs, and share in each others' celebrations and special events. It also may be necessary for newsletters, signs, and other forms of communication to be printed in the other language(s) involved, in addition to English.

Multilingual/ Multicultural Projects

"Mei Lun Yuen" is transliterated Chinese for "Garden of Beautiful Neighbors;" appropriately, it is the name of an exemplary San Francisco housing complex for senior citizens and families with modest incomes. Studio apartments and one-, three-, and four-bedroom units are available to persons whose incomes qualify for HUD assistance. Generally, the monthly charge is set at 25 percent of income. The Presbyterian Church in Chinatown, which has operated its own medical clinic and bilingual school since the mid-nineteenth century, began in 1970 to work toward the establishment of low-cost housing for the elderly. Four years later the San Francisco Redevelopment Agency approved the church as sponsor, and recommended the project to HUD. Public hearings and meetings with city and federal agencies, architects and contractors followed. Architects Associated, A.I.A., designed the complex of high-rise buildings and townhouses to provide residents with a view of the bay, and also to provide privacy without isolation. There is a central dining room for those who do not wish to prepare their own meals, plus an outdoor recreation area, and a community room. The site is downtown San Francisco, within walking distance of shopping and other conveniences, plus a tremendous number of resources representing many cultures. The complex is serviced by a professional management company, the John Stewart Company, in San Francisco. The two-page bilingual application/contract, a good example of a compact, easy-to-follow form, is reproduced in Figure C.1, Appendix C. The bilingual structure of this form is easily adaptable to the content of other housing-related forms, using two or more languages.

It should be pointed out that the needs of the manager and residents that have been discussed, particularly those in this chapter and the two preceding chapters, along with the discussions of methods and means by which these needs may be met, apply to all elderly housing situations, whether or not the residents are able to live independently. Therefore, they should be kept in mind throughout the reading of the chapter that follows.

6　Managing Semi-Independent Living

The basic difference between housing for independent living and for semi-independent living is the structure itself. Housing designed for semi-independence incorporates permanent features that accommodate supportive services, such as a food preparation center, central dining room, and some facilities for basic health care functions. Housing for semi-independent and supported living situations is distinctive because of special safety features and specifications such as the widening of doorways and corridors to accommodate wheelchairs, walkers, and prosthetic devices. Yet, as discussed in the previous chapter, there are structures designed for independent living that incorporate some of these features for optional use, to make the situation more flexible for residents who develop illnesses or infirmities. It is, of course, desirable to postpone as long as possible the need to move to a supported-living facility. Viewing an individual's state of health or disability at any one time as a point on a continuum, along which the individual may travel in either direction—i.e., worsening or recovering—it is easy to see that incorporating supportive features for optional use is conducive to more stable and predictable unit occupancy. A housing project without these structural features must depend on the availability of services to tide basically independent residents over periods of need for some support. Many of these features are worthwhile considering for any residential facility; some are mandatory for public buildings. Chapter 7 discusses them in detail.

Congregate Housing History

Historically, the service-integrated group living concept at the center of the definition of congregate housing is the original model of housing for the aged. The first such homes, begun during the nineteenth century, and sponsored and serviced by religious congregations, housed all their needy aged, in sickness and in health, and attempted to serve whatever needs they had on entry, as well as those that developed as time passed. One advantage of integrating the ill with the well is that living with a group that includes those who can live independently avoids general categorization of residents in the project as less than self-sufficient. It also provides models of capability that lend vigor and hope to the environment.

It is time that policymakers and housing developers recognize that the aging process for most is gradual and that there is an inherent responsibility to assure continued residence, if at all possible, when residents already in their seventies are admitted. We do not generally change overnight from being well to being sick and yet our past housing programs present an either-or situation: one is either completely well and able and can do quite well in housing for independent living, or one is ill and needs care in a medical facility. Between these two extremes there is a large group, estimated to be from 4 to 6 million, who, over time, as the aging process gradually takes its toll, will need assistance with the daily chores of living, even though medical supervision or care is not needed. They should be able to remain in residential environments and should be provided the sustaining services. This concept was recognized first by President Kennedy when, in 1963, he recommended to Congress a program of group living with services. No action was taken until 1970 when Congress passed the first congregate-housing act. However, because the National Nutrition Act was pending at that time, Congress provided for the cost of dining rooms and kitchens with all necessary equipment, but did not provide for the purchase, preparation, and serving of meals. Therefore, very little congregate housing resulted (Marie McGuire Thompson, "Enriching Environments for Older People," *Congregate Housing for Older People* [Lexington, Mass.: Lexington Books, D. C. Heath and Company, 1982], p. 4).

The Congregate Housing Services Act of 1978 supplied the missing element— the service subsidy—on a three-year contract basis with the housing complex, to be made available to residents in need of it. Since 1978, HUD, together with the Farmers Home Administration (FmHA), has gradually expanded its field of action from housing finance and sponsored production to include development of model congregate housing programs. FmHA has been developing small (24-unit) projects in sparsely-populated areas, and HUD has provided new Section 202 projects with five-year service packages.

Resources for Service

Two elements basic to the definition of congregate housing are its specialized structure and services. The structure of this type of housing is distinctive in that it incorporates design features that equip residents who are handicapped or disabled to function on an equal basis with those who are able-bodied. Details of those design features, as mentioned earlier in this chapter, are set forth in chapter 7.

Services, as part of the definition of congregate housing, are incorporated into the original plan, but also, as needs dictate, may be added at any point in the development or operation of the complex.

Mobile Units

Well-equipped mobile units staffed by professionals can provide basic medical care, including routine checkups, therapy, health education, health-related personal care services, and referrals to sources of specialized health care. These services can constitute the health care program offered by a congregate housing complex, or they can supplement a modest-scale in-house program. The mobile unit may be set up in the parking lot on the grounds of the housing complex, or an empty lot or wide street area can be used for this purpose. Permission for the latter, of course, must be requested from the local department of streets and sanitation, and barriers to indicate this temporary use of the area must be set up in accordance with local statutes. A single mobile unit might be scheduled to serve several housing complexes. In any case, each resident should be furnished with a printed or photocopied schedule of hours of access, showing the exact location of the mobile unit. Encouragement to have regular checkups should be a basic goal of discussions with residents, and should be emphasized in printed announcements of the service. One of the principal difficulties in treating elderly persons is a reluctance to seek health care, and even to acknowledge health-related difficulties they may be having. In many, the resulting delay can mean the difference between a condition that is still a minor problem and one that requires drastic and much more costly measures. In some, a delay can mean the difference between a condition that is treatable and one that is beyond help. Another point illustrating the need of elderly persons for regular checkups is the following:

Assuming that a change in an elderly person is due to normal aging when, in fact, it is due to disease, and therefore neglecting it, has a predictably adverse outcome for the patient. Likewise, assuming that a phenomenon of normal human aging is due to a disease and trying to treat it with drugs or surgery, is at least equally hazardous to the patient (Richard W. Besdine and Sylvia Sherwood, "Health-Care Needs of Elderly in Congregate Housing," *Congregate Housing for Older People* [Lexington, Mass.: Lexington Books, D.C. Heath and Company, 1982], p. 194).

Health Aide Training for Residents

There are times when nothing but immediate action can save a life, and there are simple measures any resident can take to help another in an emergency. Local chapters of agencies such as the Red Cross can train residents to provide emergency measures such as cardio-pulmonary resuscitation (CPR) and the Heimlich method of dislodging foreign matter from the throat or esophagus. For residents who desire further training, nursing schools and medical schools in the area can set up courses to qualify them as home health aides. Each resident should have a list of the names, phone numbers, and locations of persons who are thus qualified. A schedule might be worked out placing one on each floor of the building "on call" during specified hours.

Safety and Security

One method of 24-hour coverage which has been found effective is the employment and housing of a "custodial family" within the building or development. The family member employed on the staff of the housing complex can be a night watchman who is trained in first-aid procedures. As part of the general security system, an alarm should be installed in each dwelling unit that sounds in the manager's office, the apartment of the "buddy" or other neighbor, or in the custodial family's apartment. A resident designated as "captain" can also be assigned to each floor to act in case of emergency.

A definite emergency plan should be drawn up, distributed to each resident, and posted at the emergency annunciator board, as well as at each of the gathering-places in the building. The plan, developed with the help of the local police and fire departments, should include instructions on how to obtain prearranged medical and ambulance service, the names and phone numbers of project management personnel to notify in case of emergency, and the name and phone number of each resident family member to be contacted. The plan should also include names and phone numbers of alternate persons to be contacted in the event that the persons on the primary list cannot be reached immediately. The Medical History Card, shown as Figure C.4 in Appendix C, is an example of a succinct record card that can be posted in a convenient location, such as the reverse side of the front closet door in each unit, for quick consultation in case of emergency. The manager should schedule meetings with the residents from time to time to go over details of the plan and answer any questions they may have. The manager should also keep a file of the names, addresses, and phone numbers of the residents' personal physicians, and the names of relatives or friends they wish to have notified in case of illness or accident.

Information on health-aide training courses and other instruction in emergency care can be obtained from Manpower Development Training in Washington, D.C. Structural and design elements related to safety and security are detailed and illustrated in chapter 7.

Nutrition

Many elderly persons, particularly those who are dispirited or low on energy, are not motivated to maintain the well-balanced diet that is necessary to keep up their strength and resistance to disease. The syndrome commonly misconstrued as senility has been found in most cases to be the result, at least in part, of nutritional deficiency. Although the dwelling units in residential facilities for semi-independent living are equipped with kitchens, most also provide for central food preparation and for service in a central dining room to residents who do not wish to prepare their own food for every meal. A program of counseling on nutrition is offered along with homemaker services in many areas. The community-based "Meals on Wheels" program can deliver two meals per day (one hot, one cold) to persons who cannot prepare their own food or use the central dining room, and to persons who live in

Residents meet for lunch in the central dining room of a congregate housing complex.

HUD

complexes that do not have dining facilities. Pointers for stretching food budgets are available from organizations for the aging. Organization names and addresses are listed in Appendix A of this book. Another way to cut the cost of individual meals considerably is to equip the nearest neighborhood center or a facility in the building with kitchenware and organize a resident committee to pool funds for shopping, so that they may cook one or two meals a day, and use these mealtime get-togethers as occasions to provide instructions on nutrition and cooking.

Physical Conditioning

Because any kind of physical therapy program must be administered by a qualified person, in full knowledge of each participant's state of health, such programs must be developed in cooperation with the individuals' physicians. Community organizations can supply the kinds of physical therapists needed, and often there is a great saving in the cost of such a program per individual when a sufficient number can be served at the same location on the same schedule.

A general physical fitness program can begin with a fairly casual schedule of morning and evening walks, walks that may have a dual purpose: birdwatching, stargazing, architectural tours, for example. These may be conducted by staff members, resident committees, or by volunteers from the community. Calisthenics can be added to the schedule, and, in time, the complex may offer a variety of activities, including dance classes, square dances, and aerobics.

Home Care Programs

In most urban communities, home care programs are made available by local homemaker service agencies, health centers, and welfare departments. These programs include nursing care, physical therapy, and homemaker services. This resource can by used by the manager to help the resident bridge the gap between hospital and outpatient care.

I'm such a cripple. When I first heard about having homemaker services in my apartment, I couldn't even hook up the vacuum cleaner, so I really needed to have a cleaning lady. When I first learned of the availability of this service, I went right to the administrator of the apartments and asked how I could get involved. I love this program; my breakfast and my cleaning lady are just great. (Mrs. Blanche Jones, resident in a housing complex for the elderly).

Fitness and the Aging Process

As mentioned earlier, it is important to distinguish the changes normally associated during the aging process from changes that might occur with the onset of an illness or disability. This section will explore the normal changes that may occur during the seventh, eighth, and ninth decades of life.

Health, endurance, nutrition, and general well-being are all dependent on a common denominator—circulatory fitness. The only way to get it is via a systematic method of exercise. As a man or woman gets older, youth gradually disappears in proportion to the ebbing of the metabolism and circulation. To retain the physical capacities of youth, a person must maintain circulatory and muscular fitness. The fight is mainly to keep the capillaries open by constantly working the body. Otherwise, one will grow old prematurely (Thomas J. Cureton, director of the Physical Fitness Laboratory, the University of Illinois: 1977 report of test given to 50,000 men and women).

It is natural to feel some anxiety when physical changes occur, particularly when there is doubt as to whether the cause of a change is a threat to health or simply a result of the aging process. These anxieties can be relieved by having regular checkups, and, between them, by having a health professional—doctor, nurse, hospital administrator, or therapist—come in occasionally to give a talk to the group and answer questions about the onset of these phenomena.

Each person has an individually-set biological time clock that is affected not only by heredity but by environmental conditions and life experiences such as accidents and disease; however, there is a general chronology of changes that can be expected to take place in the human body with the advancing years. Some persons experience little or no change; others suffer pronounced losses in some body organs or functions, and, at the same time, little change, or even improvement, in others. According to gerontologist Simone de Beauvoir, the following changes characteristically take place in the aging process:

1. Motor skills lessen.
2. Decreasing ability to respond quickly to complex activities and unfamiliar demands.
3. Graying or loss of hair.
4. Skin becomes thinner and brown blotches appear.
5. Skin may become wrinkled.
6. Body becomes less sensitive to extreme heat and cold (parts can freeze or burn with only limited awareness).
7. Body becomes shorter (one to two inches) through compression of spinal discs and vertebrae.
8. Body may become stooped. It helps to walk "tall" and sit "tall."
9. Teeth may become diseased and come out.
10. Particularly with loss of teeth but often unrelated, the nose and chin become closer together.
11. Ear lobes are apt to increase in relative length.
12. The skeleton may suffer from osteoporosis, meaning that the dense part of such bones as the femur may become porous and fragile, leading to easy fractures (Simone de Beauvoir, *The Coming of Age* [New York: G.P. Putnam's Sons, 1972]).

Another chronology based on age-related changes regarded as normal should be especially helpful in determining the extent of need for special features in housing for the elderly:

1. At 20: vision becomes less sharp.
   At 50: twice as much light needed to read.
   At 80: three times as much light needed to read.
2. At 20: hearing loss begins, particularly in higher frequencies, continues throughout life.
   At 55: men's hearing loss becomes greater than women's.
   Doorbells, telephones, and voices should be low-toned.
3. At 70: taste buds may be reduced by about 45 percent, creating preference for spicy and tart foods over sweets. (James D. Manney, Jr., *Aging in Modern Society* [Ann Arbor: University of Michigan Press, 1975]).

Manney notes that some aged persons find it more difficult to keep their balance, in some the sense of smell diminishes, and in some the sense of touch is reduced. Of course, these changes do not occur to a marked extent in everyone, and where they are marked, it is not at the same age for all who are affected. For example, among persons in the retirement years, only 30 percent experience hearing loss to the extent that it can limit interaction with others. Up to 30 percent of persons *beyond the age of 80* experience diminishing ability to distinguish odors; those who do may lose interest in food. Most older persons wear glasses, and only 20 percent of the elderly population has less than adequate vision. However, the amount of time needed to focus increases with advancing age. Decreased mobility because of visual loss and consequent fear of injury can lead to feelings of isolation and depression in some persons.

Mobility can also be decreased by changes in the nervous system which can slow reaction time or reduce the sense of balance or position. This can limit even familiar activities such as using stairs.

Other biological changes which occur in older age include:

a. Dehydration, which affects the body's ability to adjust to temperature changes and also leads to dryness of skin and stiffening of joints;
b. Bones becoming brittle, breaking easily yet healing slowly, due to calcium deficiency;
c. Muscle shrinkage due to dehydration and increases in fatty tissue;
d. Heart valves losing elasticity and clogging of blood vessels, possibly resulting in poor blood circulation and an increase in blood pressure;
e. Disorders of the digestive system and urinary tract.

Even among healthy elderly persons, episodes of depression ranging in duration from several hours to several days are not uncommon. Depression is common in old age because losses and stresses occur more frequently; depression is a common reaction to loss and stress. At times, depression may be an appropriate reaction to a loss or stress. Only excessively severe or long periods of depression require medical attention . . . At times it is difficult to determine whether a person is experiencing a severe depression or manifesting symptoms of organic mental illness, since the symptoms are quite similar. In addition, the two conditions may occur simultaneously (*Characteristics of the Elderly* [Washington, D.C.: HUD, 1979]).

The standard manifestations of disease in the young are replaced in the elderly patient by one or more nonspecific but functionally devastating problems. These include loss of appetite, acute confusion, new or worsening dementia, incontinence, falls, dizziness, and failure to thrive. The appearance of any of these symptoms or signs in an elderly patient is never due to normal human aging. To attribute any to aging is to adopt an ignorant attitude and deny the patient the benefit of professional care (Richard W. Besdine and Sylvia Sherwood, "Health-Care Needs of Elderly in Congregate Housing," *Congregate Housing for Older People* [Lexington, Mass.: Lexington Books, D.C. Heath and Company, 1982], p. 195).

It is essential for the manager to understand residents' needs and symptoms. For example, if the thermostat is lowered to 65 degrees or less to conserve fuel, elderly persons—especially the old-old—can suffer accidental hypothermia, according to the National Institute on Aging. In this condition, the body temperature may fall to the point of producing cardiovascular collapse and possibly result in death. Some elderly persons are unable to maintain a healthy body temperature in a cold room; some do not perceive that the body temperature has dropped to a point well below normal. The person is cold to the touch, appears increasingly confused, and may go into a stupor or coma. The body temperature is 90 degrees or lower, and the pulse is slow. The face may be puffy or pink. Victims should be rewarmed very slowly because rapid warming can be fatal. Medical care is necessary.

Approximately 86 percent of the elderly have some type of chronic illness. This may increase the frequency of visits to the doctor as time goes on, and may require special diets, exercise, and drugs. Some of the elderly do not seek medical care because they share the widespread misapprehension that illness at their age is natural, and they expect to be ill and dependent. Other persons reinforce these feelings when they fail to encourage the elderly to seek medical aid. On the other hand, extending obviously unneeded help fosters feelings of helplessness. Chronic illness may restrict activity and may create a preoccupation with bodily needs. Most of the chronically ill, however, are not limited by illness to such a degree that they cannot live active, satisfying lives.

The Case for Congregate Housing

Congregate housing is designed to serve persons who are:

1. Frail, perhaps with a chronic illness that is under control, but not severely ill.

2. Handicapped, but not in need of institutional care.

3. Displaced, such as the single able-bodied person needing minimum shelter and services.

4. In need of minimum or occasional services.

The goal of congregate housing is to provide, as long as possible, a residential living environment rather than an institutional setting—in other words, the relative independence of a private apartment rather than the controlled environment of a bed in a hospital or nursing home. If "home" is an apartment rather than a hospital bed, a health problem—even one requiring hospitalization or nursing home care—can be regarded as a temporary interruption of the resident's lifestyle. A lifecare facility provides the resident with nursing home care on the site, when needed, along with the prospect of moving back to the private dwelling-unit on recovery.

Applicant Screening

In addition to the standard application/contract form requesting applicant information and credit references, a medical report is useful in determining the suitability of congregate housing for the applicant, and the nature and extent of the applicant's need for services. Knowing the extent of the applicant's needs also helps to determine the priority to place on the application. As mentioned in chapter 4, standardization of the application process so that the same information is required of all applicants results in a smoother operation, in the course of which no applicant will have any reason to feel singled out because of a disability or chronic illness. Medical reports for all residents should be kept in an accessible file for reference in case of a medical emergency or a change in the resident's physical or mental condition. A new medical report should accompany each renewal of the lease or other rental agreement. As mentioned earlier in this chapter, a Medical History Card should be placed unobtrusively in the designated area in each apartment, to facilitate quick and appropriate action in case of emergency. The applicant's personal physician is asked to update the card and fill out the report, detailing the history of any medical or mental illnesses, surgery, accidents, test results, treatment, and evaluation of the physical abilities and social skills needed to adjust to life in a congregate housing complex. An example of a two-page medical report form is shown in Figure C.5, Appendix C.

Priorities for Selection

Prime considerations for selection of residents are the following:

1. Date of application.
2. Need.
3. Appropriate unit size.
4. Mix of backgrounds: racial, ethnic, and religious.

Often there is a temptation to give ambulatory applicants priority over others. Admission staff personnel must take a holistic approach to each case, determining the urgency of need, and make a judgment as to what type of housing will best serve current and expected needs.

Handling Rejections

The staff should be thoroughly familiar with all the other housing alternatives for the elderly in the area, and be prepared to make referrals and recommendations on the basis of the reasons for finding another type of housing better suited to the needs of the applicant. It is sometimes desirable to make contact with the manager of a recommended facility before talking with the applicant, to make certain of the availability of the desired-size space with the necessary features and services.

Waiting List

The four elements involved in the selection process should determine priorities for the waiting list. The number of applicants it is advisable to keep on an active waiting list depends greatly on the size of the project and a reasonable expectation of turnover. Each applicant on the waiting list should be notified whenever there is an advancement in position, to determine whether or not there still is interest in being kept on the list. To be of value, the entire list should be reviewed at least semi-annually.

The Case for Supported Living

Thinking of each person's range of needs and abilities as points on a continuum, it is easy to see that as the years advance changes may occur so gradually that it is difficult for the most attentive manager to discern much difference from one day to the next unless there is an event such as an accident or catastrophic illness. At that time a reassessment of needs and abilities may result in transfer to a health care facility on either a temporary or permanent basis. Without a re-examination, it is up to the manager to discern whether or not the resident is functioning adequately in a congregate housing complex. If no available services can bring the person sufficient independence to continue living there comfortably, the manager should confer with the resident, family and friends to determine the best alternative. To the greatest extent possible, the individual should make the decision, based on the information gathered by the manager.

The dread with which most persons regard the prospect of entering a nursing home stems partially from feelings of frustration at being dependent, partially from the fear that this may be the "last stop" in their earthly journey, and partially from "horror story" headlines concerning neglect and abuse in some of those institutions. The latter represent a small percentage of the 20,000-plus nursing homes in the United States. The manager can provide the elderly applicant with reliable information on the nursing homes in the area, and can arrange a visit to allay whatever fears there may be. Stress should be placed on the health needs that the nursing home can meet, and if there is reasonable hope of doing so, the prospect of returning to independent life.

There are times when it may be wrong to keep persons out of nursing homes. There are mental conditions and physical impairments which need the expertise potentially available in such an institution. However, some persons who may need the services of a nursing home are not able to afford it. Many such persons are hidden away trying to fend for themselves against overwhelming odds (Tilman R. Smith, *In Favor of Growing Older* [Scottdale, Pa: Herald Press, 1981], p. 139).

Besides providing the needed health care facilities and the trained professional staff, the nursing home differs from independent and semi-independent living arrangements in two important respects:

1. The individual's personal space. Possession of a tangible unit of space seems almost essential for one to maintain one's identity, according to Leon A. Pastalan (*Factors Influencing the Abandonment of Private Homes by the Elderly* [Final Report for the Michigan Administration on Aging, Office of Human Development, April 30, 1977]). Although it is obviously more costly to provide private rooms, it is worth a great deal in terms of morale, pride, and peace of mind. Whether the room is private or shared, personal possessions and furnishings can be moved in to create a home-like environment with the stamp of the occupant's personality. If the room is shared, screens or room dividers can be arranged to provide privacy when desired.

2. The individual's control over schedules. Every effort should be made to provide the individual with as many choices as practicality allows. Although convenience and time of staff and management are important factors in setting schedules that apply to the residents in general, the right of residents to make decisions is important to the maintenance of morale, and should be exercised at every opportunity. If the individual's decision-making ability appears to be deteriorating, tact and care on the part of the management and staff can produce the desired result without a loss of the patient's dignity and pride.

Requirements for federal housing programs and state certification dictate many details of the construction and interior features of nursing homes, but there is room for items of decor that reflect the tastes and interests of the occupants of the facility. For example, handicrafts and other familiar ornamentation can brighten the room and make the resident feel more at home. The most prominent furnishing of the room—the hospital bed—can, on days when the occupant is not bedfast, be wheeled to a position against a wall, adjusted to a convenient level for sitting, and covered to resemble a daybed.

The volunteer, community-based social support programs and management-conducted resident activities described in previous sections of this book are as important for nursing home environments as they are for other types of elderly housing projects. Keeping in touch with the mainstream of life helps to maintain morale and to restore vigor to the resident's efforts toward recovery.

The social and physical support program should include a variety of challenges to the resident—at the level of physical stress and social responsibility that stimulates effort to achieve and improve strengths and skills—along with sufficient feedback and recognition to encourage continuing efforts. When little or no effort is required of residents, many interpret that as stemming from management's assumption that such an effort would be fruitless. Social interaction and involvement with committees and projects become even more important when the individual cannot be totally independent. Loneliness can become even more of a problem, especially when visits from family and friends are infrequent or perfunctory.

In every type of housing for the elderly, the manager and staff need to be sensitive to the feelings of persons who are experiencing loneliness and some disengagement from the mainstream. It cannot be stressed too often, that in a great many cases, frequent calls for assistance and requests to check on the functioning of fixtures or appliances, are actually, at root, cries for companionship. Rather than to limit response to a facile solution of the surface problem, the manager should convey a sense of neighborly encouragement and guidance toward involvement with specific persons or groups in the complex or surrounding area.

7 Management by Design

The basis for design and construction of housing for the elderly is accurate visualization of the needs of residents over a period of many years to come. The structure that is converted to such use or whose residents remain there until the majority have been there 15 or 20 years is likely to require alteration in the course of time in order to retain the tenants as their needs change. Prime considerations for residents are accessibility and security.

Accessibility

Hardly a residential design feature exists, from toilet bowls to kitchen cabinets, which could not be made more convenient for the elderly, as well as for everyone else. But because the public tolerates such traditional designs, the building industry has little incentive to offer mass-produced alternatives. The inevitable result is that a building constructed for the elderly or handicapped must now be custom designed. . . . Good design for practically any building is that which is responsive to the needs of older and handicapped persons. To some degree, most people are either "handicapped" or will be in the future. Ideally, they should not be required to change their living environments repeatedly to accommodate the progression of a disability (J. Buchanan Blitch, "Congregate Living: The Boarding House Alternative," *Housing for a Maturing Population* [Washington, D.C.: The Urban Land Institute, 1983]).

This view is supported by the results of a research study sponsored by the HUD Office of Policy Development and Research—findings which were used in 1980 to revise the American National Standards Institute (ANSI) A 117.1 standard. Focusing primarily on kitchen, bathroom, and circulation clearance, the report maintains that housing designed according to accessibility criteria, including tolerances and clearance for wheelchairs, does not significantly increase building costs, and can be adapted easily to use by individuals whose limitations may differ. Based on this revision of the ANSI standard, a model act—to be cited as the "Uniform Barrier-Free Design Act"—was drafted as a guide for each state. The Act contains the following definitions:

(a) "Physically handicapped" means having a temporary or permanent impairment or condition which: causes a person to walk with difficulty or insecurity; affects the sight or hearing to the extent that a person is insecure or exposed to danger; or causes faulty coordination or reduces mobility, flexibility, coordination, or perceptiveness.

(b) "Buildings and facilities" means all buildings, facilities, appurtenant grounds and curbs at crosswalks and intersections, with the exception of one- and two-family dwellings and undeveloped lands.

(c) "Architectural barriers" mean physical attributes of buildings and facilities which by their presence, absence, or design present unsafe conditions and/or deter access and free mobility for the physically handicapped in and around buildings and facilities.

Permission to reprint excerpts (Figures 3 to 18 in this book) from *Accessible Housing* (1980) has been granted by the Engineering and Codes Division, Special Office for the Handicapped, North Carolina Department of Insurance, Raleigh, N.C., as an example of a state's requirements. The following is quoted from the book:

The goals of the physically handicapped person are to have access to and throughout all buildings so they can live a more normal life and assume full responsibilities as citizens. This goal is shared by everyone.

The application of building regulations by designers and owners should take into account the safety of all occupants including the physically handicapped. Elevators are usually incapacitated early in a fire, and they are not counted as means of egress. Since the physically handicapped need assistance to negotiate stairs in exiting a building, designers and owners of buildings should consider specially designed spaces for the physically handicapped on a level where an approved ramp to grade is provided so the handicapped may exit the building without assistance. If this is not possible, designers and owners should consider the normal use of the building while the physically handicapped occupy it to assure provisions for a sufficient number of able-bodied persons readily available to assist the physically handicapped in the evacuation from such spaces down the stairs and other means of egress provided as exits in case of a fire or other emergency.

General requirements are set forth in the first five sections of the book; requirements in the remaining sections apply to specific rooms or areas. Section 5.2 of the book shows design requirements and recommendations for "Publicly-Owned Residential Projects & Privately-Owned Hotels, Motels, Residential Schools & Institutional Projects." This includes the publicly-owned multifamily housing, hospitals, and nursing homes that are discussed in this volume.

1.   Doors into the unit must provide a 32" clear opening (11x)4.3.
2.   A 1'-0" minimum clear space at the pull side of the door must be provided (11x)4.3.
3.   All door hardware must be of the type that is easy to operate.
4.   Floors within the unit must be on a continuous level or be accessible by means of a ramp, approved lift, or elevator.
5.   Controls must be located within easy reach of a seated person.
6.   Where *bathrooms* are provided they must meet the requirements outlined on pages 21 through 24.

Residential units accessible to the physically handicapped must not be segregated from other units. For example, in large apartment complexes all the units for the disabled may not be placed in one building but must be dispersed throughout the complex. This statement applies equally to the book's Section 5.2 and to Section 5.3—"Privately-Owned Residential Units for Rent or Lease." All public spaces, and five percent (minimum: one) of the residential units must meet the accessibility requirements for the appropriate property type—whether described in Section 5.2 or 5.3.

It is necessary to check the building code requirements for the state in which the housing complex is to be built. The following are North Carolina requirements mentioned in the book.

Controls such as switches, thermostats, drapery pulls, etc., must be no more than 48″ above the floor.

Entire floor area must be on one level or otherwise accessible to wheelchairs.

36″ wide door with easy-to-use handle.

Flush threshold.

Accessible walk to other accessible features: parking, other apartments, office, etc.

One 30″ wide low work surface with knee space. (Ed. note: in kitchen.)

5′0″ x 5′0″ clear floor space.

All passage doors must provide a 32″ clear opening and, preferably, have lever-type handles.

Mirror over lavatory and placed at 40″ above floor.

Walls at tubs and toilets must be reinforced to be capable of having grab bars added.

Walls in bathrooms must be at least 6′0″ apart except at tubs.

Smoke detectors are required.

Accessible Housing shows the following as recommended but not required.

Peephole at 42″ above the floor.

All closet rods adjustable to 48″ above floor.

Removable cabinet front for knee space under sink.

Side-by-side refrigerator/freezer.

Dishwasher with drop front, top controls, and roll out racks.

Range or cooktop with front or side mounted controls.

Removable cabinet front for knee space beside range.

Lavatory with single lever faucet and with clear knee space.

Controls at tub include hand-held shower head and single lever thermostatic control.

Parking Space

About 20 percent of the total of residents in housing for the elderly own and drive cars. It is important to many of these persons, as they enter elderly housing, to preserve a means of getting around independently. Typically, they use the car as long as it lasts, but do not buy a replacement. In a new building, 30 to 60 percent own and drive cars, but, with the advancing years, this percentage decreases. Space must be provided not only for these cars, but also

---

Ed. note: pages and section numbers mentioned relative to requirements refer to those in *Accessible Housing.*

for the autos, buses, vans, and other vehicles to be parked by the staff, volunteer workers, and visitors. Parking should be adjacent to the building, or underneath it. If on-the-street parking privileges are needed, but restricted, local zoning variances should be sought.

Walkways and Outdoor Sitting Space

Fencing or hand rails should be provided along sidewalks, particularly where the ground slopes. Walkways and patios should be made of solid pavement rather than flagstone, slate, or gravel. Outdoor sitting areas are used and enjoyed by most elderly residents; they add a much-needed dimension to apartment living, and the accessibility of a place to rest outdoors stimulates residents to be more active physically and socially. Benches, chairs, and tables can be provided for games such as cards, checkers, and chess. Equipment for active recreation, such as badminton, shuffleboard, horseshoes, and swimming can be added as interest is expressed and resources permit.

Lighting and Colors: Outdoors and Indoors

Because elderly eyes need more light in order to see well, it is important to provide adequate lighting everywhere in the housing complex, especially along walkways, ramps, halls, stairwells, and elevators. Photo cells, rather than timers, should be installed for proper illumination on days that are overcast.

Wherever possible, the object to be grasped, such as a railing or door handle, should be a color that contrasts with its framework or background. In most structures, floors as viewed from stairtops and elevators look alike; therefore, it is a good idea to provide a clue at each of those points, such as a different wall color for each floor, to prevent confusion and disorientation. Intense, distinctive tones should be used: deep blue rather than pale blue, plum rather than lavender, gold rather than beige. Braille codes denoting the floor number can be installed on the undersides of hall support railings for guidance.

Building Entrance and Interior Doors

Where stairs are used to gain entrance to the building, a ramp should also be provided, with handrails on both sides 32 inches above the nosings. At least one handrail must extend 1 foot 6 inches beyond the top and bottom risers. A planted area should frame this access point. The entrance itself should be set back from the face of the building, with doors deeply enough recessed so that the person approaching them can take shelter from the weather, if need be, while digging for a key or buzzing for entry. The photograph on the cover of this book shows a well-lighted building entrance, with supportive handrails extending from the doors throughout the corridors. A sidewalk ramp and nonskid tiles afford easy entrance.

Doors should be substantial, but not so heavy that they are difficult to push open, and they should be balanced. Automatic doors, wherever feasible, are a convenience for the disabled. Doorstops should be adjusted to permit slow and easy passage. Door sills should be eliminated at the main entrance, and at entrances to apartments, rooms, and elevators. In lieu of doorknobs, which can be difficult for stiffening or painful fingers to manipulate, door levers should be installed. All doors should bear easy-to-read identification, including a braille equivalent. For persons who lack coordination stamina, or use of the lower extremities, doors within the dwelling-unit might be replaced with curtains, sliding doors, or hinged, partitioned folding doors.

Corridors and Floors

Width of the corridor should allow two wheelchairs sufficient room to pass one another, and also to make a 180-degree turn. Those who rely on walking aids need 34 to 36 inches of width. Carpeting can cause problems, for wheelchairs particularly, but it does absorb sound, and it provides some insulating warmth—besides giving the area a more homelike setting. If used, the carpeting should be tightly woven, low-pile, and installed without padding so that wheelchairs do not bog down in it. Dense indoor/outdoor carpeting and cushioned, textured tile are possible solutions; they are easy to clean, require no transitional stripping, and have nonslip surfaces that do not retard the movement of a wheelchair or walker. Cushioned vinyl and tile are recommended for the area around the toilet. Smooth tiles and slick floors are hazards to those who have difficulty in lifting, bending, reaching, turning, or kneeling. Throw rugs also are hazards, unless they are firmly taped down. Any rug used should have a nonskid back. All floors that are not carpeted should be finished with a nonslip surface. However, residents who suffer from arthritis need the warmth provided by carpeting. The problem cited most often by elderly tenants is the difficulty they have in cleaning flooring or carpeting; many need help with this. A handrail should run the complete length of the corridor, and there should be a rail or wedge at the baseboard level to prevent wheelchair damage.

Electrical Outlets and Lighting in Units

Drawings and specifications for the units should clearly show the location of each electrical outlet, and the electrical contractor should not be allowed to deviate from these positions. All outlets and switches should be placed waist-high so that they are accessible from a wheelchair, and do not require that a person who is standing bend over to reach them. Blind persons use many electrical devices, and therefore need a greater number of outlets than do most sighted residents. Outlets should be placed to the front and side of counters—never on the wall above countertops, and never in corners. No heavy furniture should be placed in front of an outlet. Persons who lack upper-extremity skills can use a plugged-in push cart that has its own outlets for small appliances. Persons who are deaf can use special visual signals—preferably in every room—on a low-voltage door bell system. Those who are deaf and also blind can use a fan or odor-generating device to replace the audible or visual signal. Large, round plugs should be used. Changing bulbs is a problem for those who have limited vision, those who have upper or lower extremity limitations, those who lack coordination, and those who have difficulty handling and fingering objects; these residents need human assistance. Many with limited motor skills prefer individual task lights for tables and desks; some prefer remote control switches for general lighting. For those with visual problems, a sensory device can be used to tell whether lights are on or off, and all switch identification should be accompanied by a version in braille. There are special switches for those whose upper extremities are weak or impaired. A control panel may be installed to enable the handicapped resident to operate the light switches.

Elevators

Elevator doors that snap shut quickly force persons to enter faster than is possible for many who are disabled. There are elevators equipped with special photosensitive doors which close only on a 30-second delay. Controls are located within range of persons seated in a wheelchair, and the car is large enough for a wheelchair to turn around. The elevator should be equipped with an automatic leveling device to ensure that the platform lines up with the floor level. Persons whose use of lower extremities is limited can use a stick to reach the control buttons. Those with visual limitations need braille floor numbers beside the appropriate buttons, and an auditory signal to indicate the number of the floor reached. A person using a walker should use a cart to transport items rather than to hand-carry them into the elevator. Elevators should not be used in case of fire. Persons who cannot use stairs—and live above the ground floor—must depend on human assistance.

Steps/Stairs

Because stairs are difficult for many disabled persons to manage, and impossible for others, it has been suggested that they be eliminated entirely, and replaced by ramps and elevators. However, stairs must be provided as emergency exit routes, especially in case of fire. Persons whose physical condition permits the use of stairs should be encouraged to use them, as they constitute a good source of nonstrenuous, regular exercise.

Telephone

Pushbutton/touchtone phones and punched-card systems can solve problems many persons have in dialing. Speaker phones can help persons with limited motor skills. Large numbers and braille numbers can help those whose vision is impaired. Placement of phones, including wall phones, should be within easy reach of those in wheelchairs. Cords should be long enough to enable the resident to sit comfortably while using the phone. Primary location should be the bedroom; extensions in kitchenette and bath are helpful, especially in case of emergency. Visual signals are available for those who cannot hear the phone ring. Provision can be made in the phone line for an emergency button which can activate individual warning lights in the administrative office or in the local police station.

Interior Walls and Windows

More severe wear is given to walls by persons using wheelchairs or walking aids. Protective, mar-resistant wainscots, rails at baseboard level, and rounded corners can help minimize damage. Cleaning can be a problem for persons with impaired visual or motor skills. Long-handled cleaning devices and smooth, washable paint or wall coverings can make walls easier to maintain. Most disabled persons require help in cleaning walls.

The window is an important design element; the view enlarges the environment beyond the confines of the dwelling unit—but many residents need help with window cleaning. Again, long-handled cleaning tools can enable the resident to do a good deal of the job, but corners and small panes require leverage difficult to achieve with these devices. Windows should be placed away from corners, to provide easier access. Special two-way tilt windows enable the resident to wash the exterior as well as the interior side of the pane. The window sill should be low enough to enable a person seated in a wheelchair to view the outdoors. The area beneath it should be uncluttered so that residents in wheelchairs can pull up to it to enjoy the scene and the fresh air. Ring-type pulls and handles should be used for opening and closing. If the windows cannot be opened, special intake fans can be used to bring in the fresh air. Windows should lock and slide easily. Electrically operated tracks for drapes and curtains can be installed for the convenience of persons whose visual or motor abilities are limited.

Bookcases

Wall space should be provided for adjustable shelving for books and other reference aids. To house Braille books, 12 or 13 inches in height should be allowed; the ends of the shelves should be closed. For persons with limited motor skills, work desk and book shelves might be combined in one unit. Height of the shelves provided for persons with upper or lower extremity difficulties should be 32 to 42 inches, a convenient level to reach from a sitting position.

Living Room/Entertaining

Furniture in a living room or entertainment area should be arranged so that there is an area five feet square wherein a person in a wheelchair can make a full turn. If the resident is limited in skills of the upper extremities, the radio, stereo, and television set can be adapted to operation with a splint or mouth stick. Walls should be soundproofed to the extent possible. A pass-through between the kitchen and living/entertaining area saves much time and effort.

Kitchen

The sink and related bottom cabinetry can be adjusted to the height enabling the resident to wash dishes or prepare food while seated in a wheelchair. A stainless steel sink is recommended, with waste and supply plumbing as far as possible out of the way of the wheelchair, with under-sink cabinet doors, curtains, or shutters, which may be added or removed as chores are begun or finished. Special faucets can be adapted to different disabilities; a single-control faucet with a long-handled lever works well. For those who have difficulty moving their heads, lifting, bending, reaching, turning, or kneeling, a faucet that can be controlled with a mouth stick should be installed. For persons limited in use of the lower extremities, faucets can be installed on the side instead of in the rear of the sink; in this case it is best to use a special chair, and to eliminate the undersink cabinet. The underside of the sink must be covered, however, to prevent burns from hot-water pipes. Braille markings on faucets and reusable braille labels on food cans and packages help the visually impaired.

Kitchen cabinets often turn out to be cumbersome for able-bodied persons to use, as well as for the disabled. Pull-out, fold-down shelving that can be added as needed would be helpful. The resident can use lazy susans and special racks and "grabbers" to store and retrieve items. A walk-in pantry with shallow, adjustable shelving should allow space for wheelchair entry. Wall cabinetry should be built in at a height within the reach of the wheelchair-bound, with access made by ring-type pull hardware, rather than by knobs or recessed grab edges. Slide-out shelves and magnetic catches can be helpful to those who rely on walkers, and those whose motor skills are limited, but magnetic catches cannot be used by those who wear pacemakers. Persons with limited coordination and stamina, and those with upper- and lower-extremity difficulties, can brace themselves against bottom cabinets; those cabinets should be spaced to allow wheelchair access. Wheelchair shelving height range is 32 to 36 inches for optimum reach. Shelving should have closed ends to keep items from being pushed off, and the surfaces should be easy to clean. Hooks should be added for large spoons. A rack in a narrow cupboard—not at head level—should be installed for storing pots and pans.

If adjustable countertops that can be raised or lowered between approximately 28 and 40 inches from the floor cannot be provided, then space for an adjustable worktable should be allowed. Pull-out or dropleaf workboards can enlarge the available space. A permanent chopping block should be installed permanently near the sink or stove. All surfaces should be easy to clean, and accessible with "grabbers." Wherever possible, corners should be rounded.

There should be a variety of utility drawers, some deep, some shallow, with easy sliding mechanism, preferably in modular design for easy interchangeability. Drawers, though removable, should have a stop mechanism, and should be installed at a level to be reached comfortably from a sitting position; the lowest should be at least one foot off the floor. Drawer pulls should be the ring type. Persons with lower-extremity difficulty should have drawers accessible from the side rather than the front. Compartments for drawers are especially helpful to those with limited vision.

Because refrigerators are not built in, each resident can choose the configuration most suitable for the particular needs involved. In general, refrigerators should be the frost-free variety, with shelves that are adjustable—

some sliding—and large pull handles. Doors should open 180 degrees and require minimal pull to open. An automatic ice maker is needed by those who have difficulty with motor skills. Persons who are visually impaired need a tactile "map" to indicate location of types of items, plus a tactile marking for the "defrost" indicator.

An all-electric self-cleaning stove/oven with childproofed front pushbutton controls (with braille or other embossed designation for the visually impaired) is recommended. Ring-type handles should open oven doors easily; racks should slide easily, but have stops to keep them from falling out. Space for either a combination stove/oven or separate stove and built-in oven should include adequate clearance for wheelchair passage and "roll-under."

Wheelchair space must be planned carefully around the dining table also. To eliminate the problem of table legs getting in the way, the table can be mounted on a pedestal, or wall-mounted and, to liberate more space, dropleaf. Some of the persons whose upper extremity skills are limited prefer to use a card table. Those who have motor skill difficulties often prefer to use a lapboard for dining.

Installation of a well-designed dishwasher, well adapted for use by the disabled, appears to be warranted, because of the difficulty many disabled persons have in washing dishes by hand and in using standard-design dishwashers. Adaptations needed to equip the dishwasher for such use are as follows:

1. Side-opening door.
2. Pushbutton controls on front but not in door.
3. Lights to indicate cycle and operator.
4. Braille designations and large lettering to designate controls.
5. Revolving racks.
6. "Potscrubbers" feature to minimize need for hand-rinsing.

Garbage and trash disposal present problems to those who are confined to a wheelchair or otherwise disabled. This chore can be made easier by installing a garbage/trash chute, on each floor, or providing an accessible garbage room at the end of each corridor. The door to each of these must be easily operable from a sitting position. A trash compactor and a sink disposer in the kitchen with a large sink bowl would also constitute supports for the individual's ability to live independently.

Bathroom

The bathroom walls should be reinforced so that grab bars may be installed without weakening their structure. Height of the bathroom sink should be made adjustable; there should be adjacent countertop space. Base cabinets should be removable to accommodate wheelchairs. Faucets, like those in kitchens, should be the single-control type. A large mirror—perhaps reaching from vanity top to ceiling—should be hung over the vanity, except for those who have visual difficulties; they should have a big eye mirror that is not placed over vanity, sink, or other fixture. For those who have problems with motor skills, the wall mirror should be hung at a 45-degree tilt.

There is no one design solution to the many problems that confront the disabled in the tub and shower. At a minimum, there should be a shower/tub combination, with single-lever control reachable from a sitting position. Grab bars and slip-resistant surfaces are essential, and the shower should be adaptable to hand-held use. Where it is feasible, it is desirable to have a four-foot-square shower stall (large enough to accommodate a wheelchair and a second person) with a fold-down seat built into the wall, and the shower head on a flexible hose. For those with upper-extremity problems, controls should have an on/off button, and shower curtains should be substituted for shower doors. For individuals who have extreme limitations on motor skills, a hydraulic lift may be installed. Those who have difficulty in manipulating cleaning materials can fill the tub with the cleaning agent, and then use a long-handled mop to do the scrubbing. Visually-limited persons may wish to do this also, because using scouring powder can diminish their tactile sensitivity.

The toilet should be placed far enough from the walls to permit lateral transfer from a wheelchair. Special seats or adjustable seats can adjust the height of the fixture to a comfortable level. The flush handle should be easy to operate, and placed within easy reach. There should be an automatic shut-off for water; many persons who experience hearing loss cannot tell when it stops. The paper roll holder should be placed within easy reach at a point where it will not interfere with the operation of a wheelchair.

Bedroom

Beds generally can be adapted by the user to fit specific needs, and placed so that the view through the window is visible from the bed. Space around the bed should be large enough to accommodate a wheelchair. An orthopedic mattress or bed board can mitigate some types of back problems. The bed can be raised to facilitate making it, or lowered to permit a person with lower-extremity difficulties to sit on it while putting braces on. A person who relies on walking aids can make the bed while sitting on it by putting the sheets and blankets at the bottom and then pulling them up. Individuals who have difficulty turning their heads, reaching, bending, turning, or kneeling can use mouth stick or voice controls to operate lights, appliances and drapes.

Many persons—disabled or not—cite inadequate storage space as a major problem. Ample space should be provided, with adjustable shelves and rods. Sliding or folding doors with pull-type handles in lieu of knobs, and sliding or pull-out shelves, can help the resident organize possessions and place them where retrieval will be convenient. The interior of the closet should be lighted, with controls on the wall outside it, within wheelchair reach.

Laundry Room

There should be a centrally-located laundry room, with barrier-free access, at least 10 washers and dryers for each 100 apartments, and space for folding tables and ironing boards. Some tables should be wheelchair height. The floor should be uniformly sloped for drainage. Disabled persons can use baskets on wheels to transport laundry. A small lounge adjacent to the laundry room should provide a view of the machines. Washers and dryers should be the front-loading type, with pushbutton controls and coin slots at front, and labels that have adjacent translations into braille. Doors should open 180 degrees, swinging to one side. Placement of machines should be side by side rather than stacked. Aisles between machines should be wide enough for wheelchair passage. For the benefit of persons with hearing loss, there should be signal lights to indicate cycles and also to indicate any malfunction. A ring-type handle or sculptured handle can help persons with motor skill limitations. One ironing board should be permanently affixed in the laundry room for every 50 apartments. The board should be adjustable to minute gradations in height. Most residents prefer to iron while seated. Tape can be affixed to the "average" setting on the iron to help visually-impaired persons. A device can be attached to the cord to keep it tangle-free.

Recreation

Common recreational activities offer an opportunity to integrate persons who are able-bodied with those who are disabled. Adapting the recreational facilities to accommodate the disabled, in most instances, also makes them more convenient for usage by others. For example, providing space for wheelchair passage opens up space that results in more freedom of movement for everyone in the room. Tables should be adjustable in height or varied in height. Sometimes a "compromise" table height can be found that falls within various ranges of needs. Tables with pedestal legs allow wheelchair "rollunder." The arrangement of furniture and equipment should be kept constant for the benefit of the visually impaired who memorize these layouts. A variety of activities should be accessible, for example, billiards, cards, ping pong, arts and crafts, checkers and chess. To make use of these facilities, some persons will have to have special adaptive devices, such as braille playing cards or a telescopic mouth stick for painting.

Distance and barriers to wheelchair and walking-aid travel are problems that make it difficult for the disabled to go beyond the housing complex for recreation. If recreational activities are planned for an outside facility, it is best to select the one closest to the complex, and to provide extra help for the visually impaired who have not had the opportunity to become familiar with the arrangement of furniture and equipment in the other building.

Accessibility and the Seeing-Eye Dog

Beginning in 1975, the HUD programs and policies with regard to the handicapped were limited to the requirement that HUD multifamily housing developed for the elderly must have 10 percent of all dwelling units accessible to the disabled. The specific accessibility requirements contained in the HUD Minimum Property Standards (MPS) for such dwellings are minimal and primarily consider persons who have physical limitations, specifically those confining them to wheelchairs. No requirements for sensory disabilities (hearing and seeing disorders) are contained in the MPS, despite the fact that some deaf persons depend on trained Hearing Dogs. However, housing denial that is based on a sensory disability is a discriminatory practice. Increasingly, psychologists and psychiatrists find pet ownership to be therapeutic for elderly persons—especially those who live alone. Many rental units have firm "no pets" policies. Such a policy cannot apply to a visually impaired person who needs a Seeing-Eye dog as a sensory aid, and there is a question as to whether it could apply to a person whose pet is part of prescribed therapy. Because a Seeing-Eye dog is needed to make the premises accessible to the individual, provision must be made to accommodate them both in a dwelling-unit of the individual's choice, whether that unit is on the first floor or any other floor in the housing complex. The resident is responsible for the dog's behavior at all times—including passage through the corridors and elevators in the building, and outdoors; these dogs are so well trained, along with their owners, that they can be relied on to be good neighbors. The process of walking the dog can be a problem in an urban area where no landscaping exists. One solution can be to advise the resident to train the dog to use storm drains. The manager can ask the local fire department to treat the drains with lime and flush them down regularly. Pet Parks can be created in a rural or garden setting. If there are times that the dog's needs cannot be taken care of outdoors, there is a biodegradable sling that will fit a dog for excretory purpose; when used, it can be folded and easily disposed of, in the same manner as a baby's disposable diaper.

Security

Sensitivity in security indoctrination is essential. Security briefings should be handled in a manner that will develop awareness of the need for caution without creating unnecessary apprehension. It is an ongoing responsibility of management to keep the residents informed of all security measures in operation in the building and on the grounds of the housing project. Concern for their neighbors' well-being should be encouraged, and residents must be advised as to what to do in case of emergency: how and to whom to report accidents, crimes, illness, and other exigencies. The importance of promptness in reporting suspicious activities on the grounds or nearby streets should be stressed. Residents must be instructed on the proper use of alarm buttons, annunciator systems, door viewers (peep holes), and door chains.

Limited Access

Limiting access to a housing project for the elderly is usually not difficult, provided that the lobby door is monitored by visual observation or by an annunciator system. The lobby, in most complexes an extension of the lounge or social room, should be visible to any resident sitting there or participating in group activities. Sitting space and furniture should be provided in the lobby to enable residents to congregate informally, and, incidentally, observe the entry into the lobby. All other doors, such as service, fire, or stairwell, should be kept locked from the outside. Any doors not needed for entry into the building should not have any hardware (door handles or knobs) on the outside. Residents should be instructed to use only the lobby door for entry or departure. If a door is provided for easy access from the parking area, it should be monitored. Apartment doors should have deadbolt locks and wide-angled peepholes. In garden apartments and row houses, not only should doors be similarly equipped, but also first-floor windows should have effective locking devices and/or protective security screening.

Mail

Mail is one of the most sensitive areas in resident-management relations. Sometimes a person who fails to receive expected letters suspects management or other residents of tampering with the mail. Designing the mail room so that it is accessible only from the rear for loading by the mailman alleviates this concern. Mailboxes should be visible to residents in or near the lobby. Mailboxes in garden apartments should be constructed as closely as possible to vandalproof. They should be highly visible from the street, and residents should be encouraged to be present at the time that Social Security and Welfare Assistance checks are delivered by the mailman. A more efficient method is to have checks directly deposited to a participating bank automatically each month. In row houses, mail slots should be provided through the door and designed so as to prevent access to the mail and even to prevent the doorknob's being turned from the outside. If possible, and if the residents wish it, arrangements might be made to have the mail delivered to the management office where it can be safeguarded until called for by the residents.

Parking Lots

Pilferage and vandalism of automobiles in the parking area is one of the more common problems reported by persons in housing for the elderly. Precautions to be taken include adequate lighting, frequent police patrol, and high visibility of the area from the lounge or social room, and from the residents' apartments. Mugging and purse-snatching can occur just outside the building and in nearby streets. It is important in designing and landscaping the area to avoid creating places where a criminal can hide behind trees, shrubs, walls, or building projections. Residents should be encouraged to walk in groups whenever possible, and avoid venturing out alone.

Children

The presence of children unsupervised by adults can disturb elderly persons in garden apartment developments and in housing projects that have landscaped areas for outdoor relaxation and recreation. This occurs when children use the project grounds as a shortcut to school or other destinations, and also when grandchildren of residents roam the grounds and corridors. Usually, the presence of the children is not a threat to safety and security, but some residents may react to it as though it were. In any case, there is a risk involved in permitting children to enter the premises without supervision; for their own protection against possible accidents and injury in coping with an unfamiliar environment, supervision should be a requirement for entry. Management should be aware of this as a potential problem, and effect appropriate rules for accommodating visiting children as guests in the building, while keeping others out of the area.

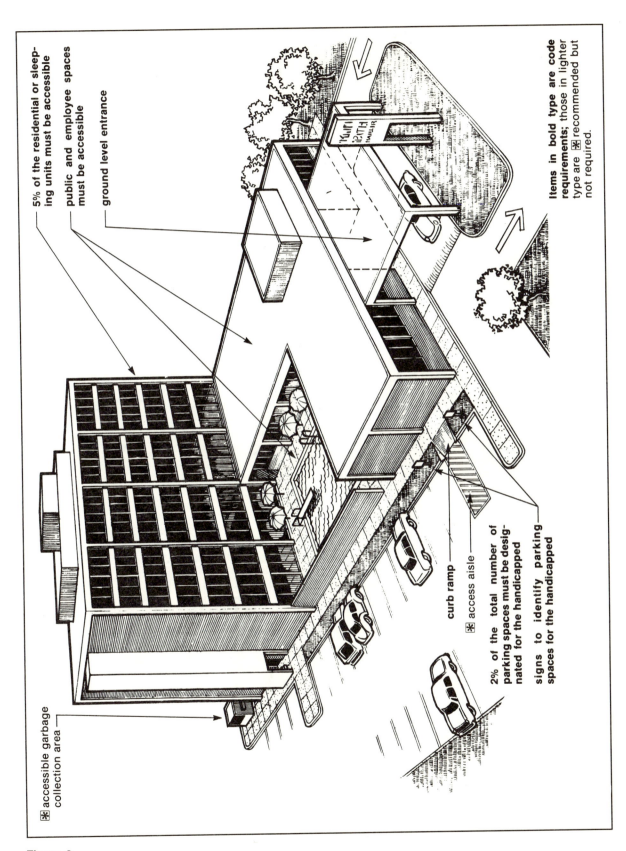

5% of the residential or sleep-ing units must be accessible

public and employee spaces must be accessible

ground level entrance

Items in **bold type are code requirements**; those in lighter type are ✳ recommended but not required.

✳ accessible garbage collection area

curb ramp

✳ access aisle

2% of the total number of parking spaces must be desig-nated for the handicapped

signs to identify parking spaces for the handicapped

Figure 3.
Site Considerations

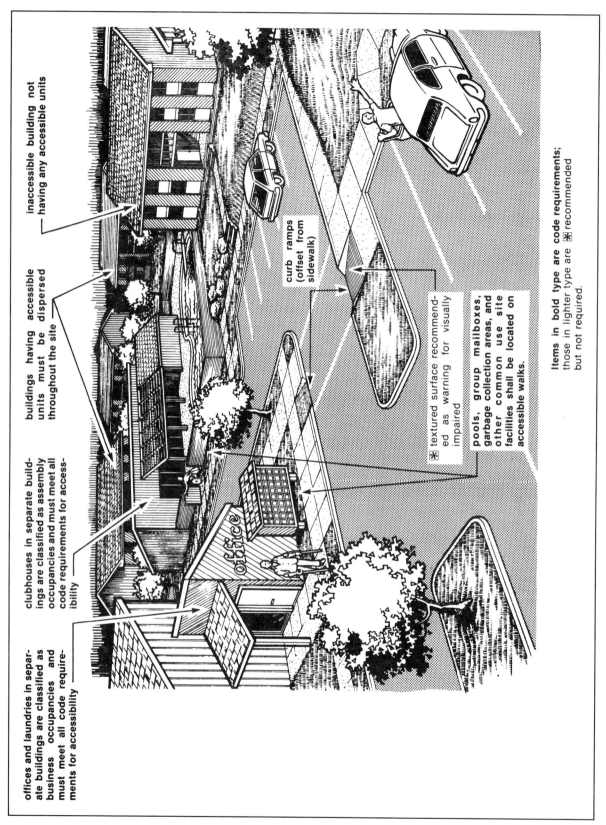

inaccessible building not having any accessible units

buildings having accessible units must be dispersed throughout the site

clubhouses in separate buildings are classified as assembly occupancies and must meet all code requirements for accessibility

offices and laundries in separate buildings are classified as business occupancies and must meet all code requirements for accessibility

curb ramps (offset from sidewalk)

✳ textured surface recommended as warning for visually impaired

pools, group mailboxes, garbage collection areas, and other common use site facilities shall be located on accessible walks.

Items in **bold type are code requirements**; those in lighter type are ✳ recommended but not required.

Figure 4.
Site Considerations
(continued)

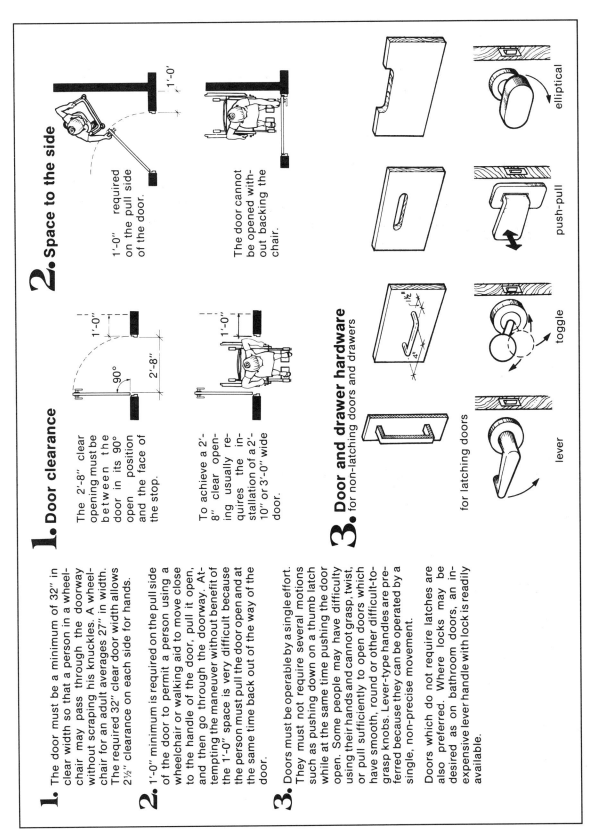

1. Door clearance

1. The door must be a minimum of 32" in clear width so that a person in a wheelchair may pass through the doorway without scraping his knuckles. A wheelchair for an adult averages 27" in width. The required 32" clear door width allows 2½" clearance on each side for hands.

2. 1'-0" minimum is required on the pull side of the door to permit a person using a wheelchair or walking aid to move close to the handle of the door, pull it open, and then go through the doorway. Attempting the maneuver without benefit of the 1'-0" space is very difficult because the person must pull the door open and at the same time back out of the way of the door.

2. Space to the side

3. Door and drawer hardware
for non-latching doors and drawers

3. Doors must be operable by a single effort. They must not require several motions such as pushing down on a thumb latch while at the same time pushing the door open. Some people may have difficulty using their hands and cannot grasp, twist, or pull sufficiently to open doors which have smooth, round or other difficult-to-grasp knobs. Lever-type handles are preferred because they can be operated by a single, non-precise movement.

Doors which do not require latches are also preferred. Where locks may be desired as on bathroom doors, an inexpensive lever handle with lock is readily available.

Figure 5.
General Requirements

1. Walks serving accessible units and connecting them with other accessible facilities must:

   a. be at least 48" wide,
   b. be no steeper than 1 in 12 (8.33%),
   c. provide a continuous common surface having no bump or abrupt change in level greater than ½", and
   d. have handrails if the slope exceeds 1 in 20 (5%).

2. Where walks cross curbs, streets, or driveways, they must blend to a common level with the street or have curb ramps. Curb ramps must be at least 40" wide and slope no more than 1 in 12 (8.33%).

3. Two percent (2%) of the total number of parking spaces provided, or a minimum of one, must be designated for disabled people. These spaces must be a minimum of 12'-6" wide and have above parking level signs.

   An economical acceptable alternative is to install standard width spaces separated by a 5'-0" wide access aisle.

4. A ramp must:

   a. be at least 4'-0"" wide.
   b. have one handrail if it slopes more than 1 in 20 (5%) and have no drop-offs at the edge,
   c. have handrails on both sides if it drops off on either side,
   d. have handrails which extend at least 1'-0" horizontally beyond the slope at each end, and
   e. have a level platform at top, bottom, wherever it changes direction, and every 30' if it is very long.

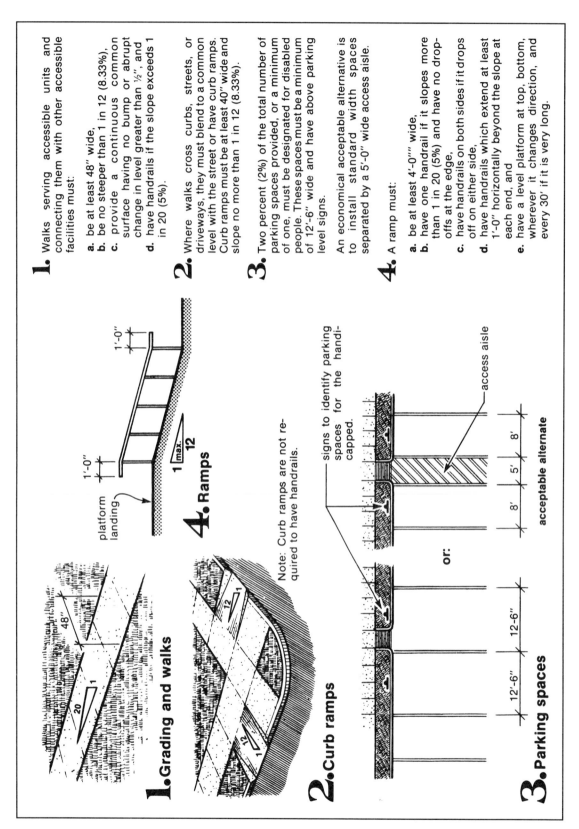

1. Grading and walks

2. Curb ramps

Note: Curb ramps are not required to have handrails.

4. Ramps

platform landing

1 max. / 12

3. Parking spaces

signs to identify parking spaces for the handicapped.

access aisle

acceptable alternate

or:

Figure 6.
General Requirements
(continued)

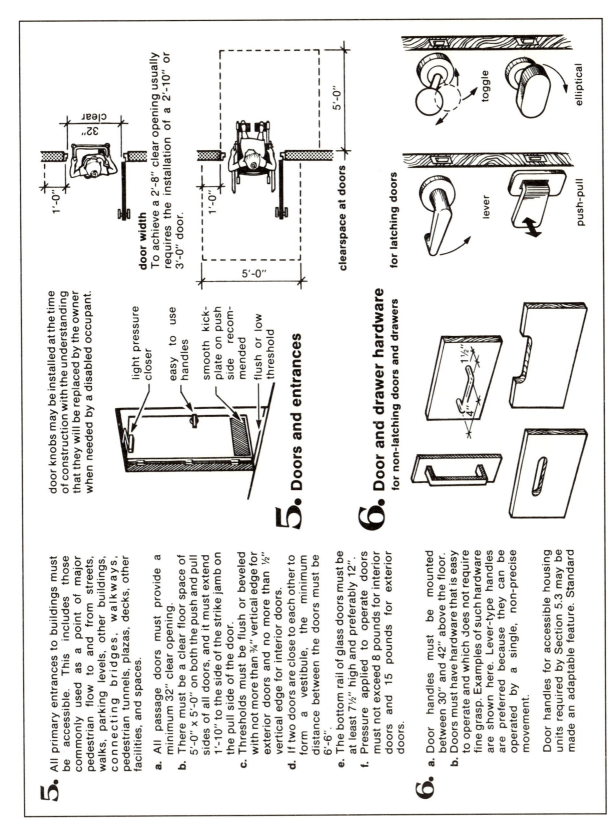

5. All primary entrances to buildings must be accessible. This includes those commonly used as a point of major pedestrian flow to and from streets, walks, parking levels, other buildings, connecting bridges, walkways, pedestrian tunnels, plazas, decks, other facilities, and spaces.

a. All passage doors must provide a minimum 32" clear opening.

b. There must be a clear floor space of 5'-0" x 5'-0" on both the push and pull sides of all doors, and it must extend 1'-10' to the side of the strike jamb on the pull side of the door.

c. Thresholds must be flush or beveled with not more than ¾" vertical edge for exterior doors and no more than ½" vertical edge for interior doors.

d. If two doors are close to each other to form a vestibule, the minimum distance between the doors must be 6'-6".

e. The bottom rail of glass doors must be at least 7½" high and preferably 12".

f. Pressure applied to operate doors must not exceed 8 pounds for interior doors and 15 pounds for exterior doors.

6. a. Door handles must be mounted between 30" and 42" above the floor.

b. Doors must have hardware that is easy to operate and which does not require fine grasp. Examples of such hardware are shown here. Lever-type handles are preferred because they can be operated by a single, non-precise movement.

Door handles for accessible housing units required by Section 5.3 may be made an adaptable feature. Standard door knobs may be installed at the time of construction with the understanding that they will be replaced by the owner when needed by a disabled occupant.

light pressure closer

easy to use handles

smooth kick-plate on push side recommended

flush or low threshold

5. Doors and entrances

6. Door and drawer hardware
for non-latching doors and drawers

door width
To achieve a 2'-8" clear opening usually requires the installation of a 2'-10" or 3'-0" door.

32" clear
1'-0"

5'-0"
1'-0"
5'-0"

clearspace at doors

for latching doors

lever
push-pull
toggle
elliptical

1½"
4"

Figure 7.
General Requirements
(continued)

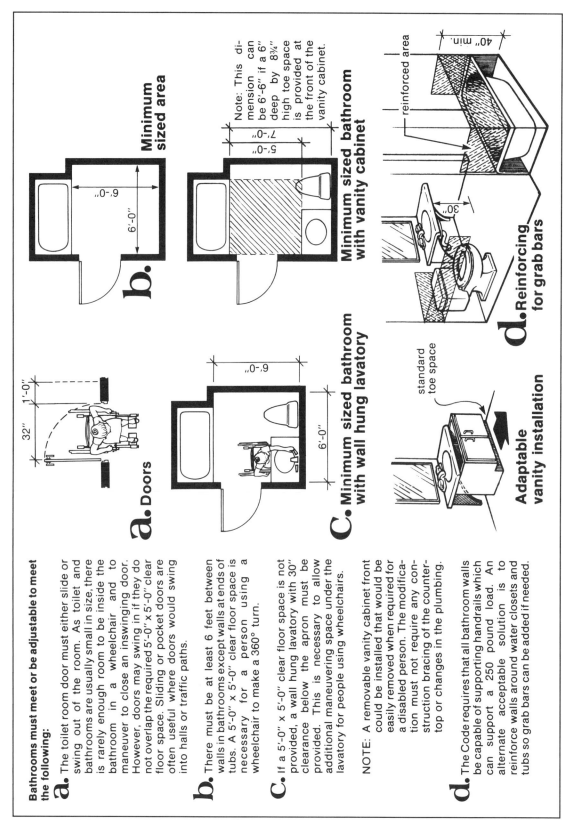

Bathrooms must meet or be adjustable to meet the following:

a. The toilet room door must either slide or swing out of the room. As toilet and bathrooms are usually small in size, there is rarely enough room to be inside the bathroom in a wheelchair and to maneuver to close an inswinging door. However, doors may swing in if they do not overlap the required 5'-0" x 5'-0" clear floor space. Sliding or pocket doors are often useful where doors would swing into halls or traffic paths.

b. There must be at least 6 feet between walls in bathrooms except walls at ends of tubs. A 5'-0" x 5'-0" clear floor space is necessary for a person using a wheelchair to make a 360° turn.

c. If a 5'-0" x 5'-0" clear floor space is not provided, a wall hung lavatory with 30" clearance below the apron must be provided. This is necessary to allow additional maneuvering space under the lavatory for people using wheelchairs.

NOTE: A removable vanity cabinet front could be installed that would be easily removed when required for a disabled person. The modification must not require any construction bracing of the countertop or changes in the plumbing.

d. The Code requires that all bathroom walls be capable of supporting handrails which can support a 250 pound load. An alternate acceptable solution is to reinforce walls around water closets and tubs so grab bars can be added if needed.

Figure 8.
Bathrooms

e. Mirrors

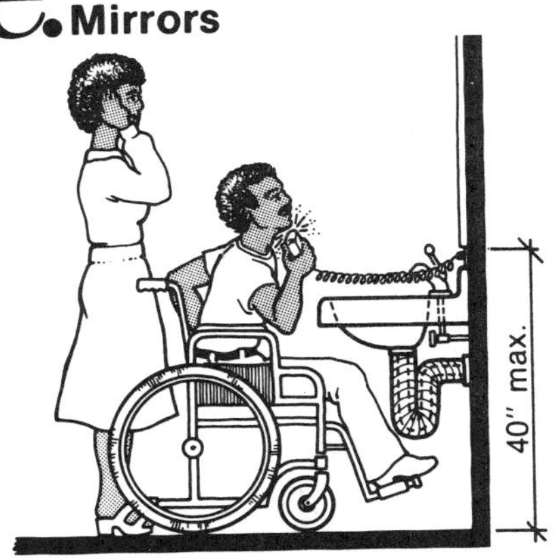

When provided, mirrors placed over lavatories must be mounted so that the bottom edge is no higher than 40" above the floor to permit a small person or someone seated in a wheelchair to see to comb their hair, shave, apply make-up, etc. If the mirror is tall enough, it will also work well for standing people. Tilt mirrors are discouraged because when in a position to be usable by a person in a wheelchair they do not work well for a standing person. Some tilt mirrors are also subject to vandalism because of moving parts.

Caution: Electrical outlets should be located within the allowable reach range, but at the same time they must be located where they cannot get wet.

f. Towel bars

Where provided, towel storage racks as well as towel bars should be mounted so that the bottom edge is no higher than 40" from the floor and preferably is not on the wall behind the toilet.

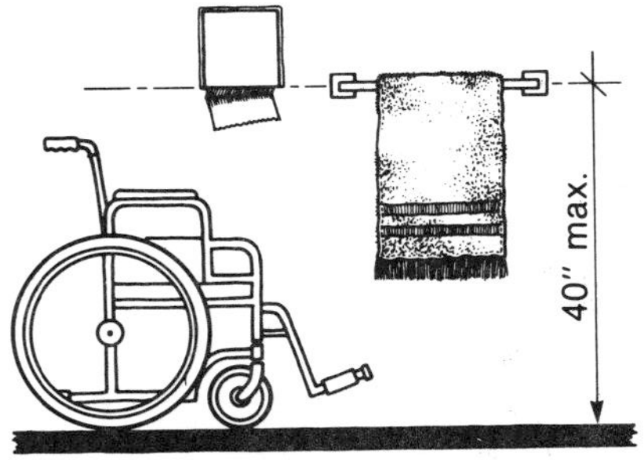

g. Insulated lavatory piping

The water temperature at lavatories must not exceed 120°F, or exposed hot water lines and drains must be insulated to prevent burns on persons with little or no sensation in their legs. If lavatories are placed in vanities with covered fronts, the water temperature does not need to be reduced nor do the pipes require insulating. If wall-hung lavatories or lavatories placed in countertops without fronts are installed, some protective measures must be taken. To avoid unsightly exposed wrapped pipes, a mixing valve with temperature limiting device could be installed.

The piping does not prevent a person in a wheelchair from pulling up under the lavatory. Neither of these solutions require insulation nor reduced water temperature.

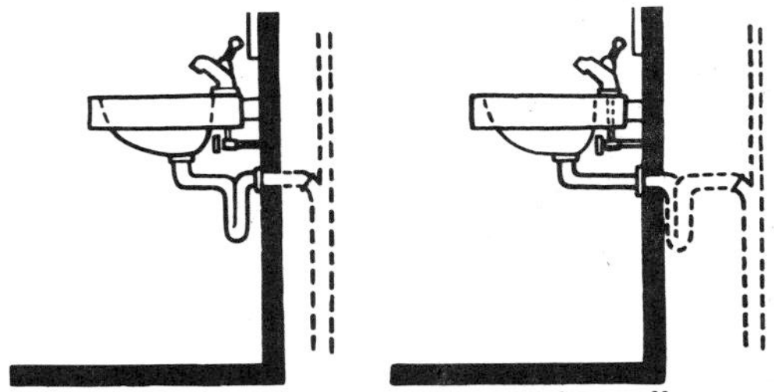

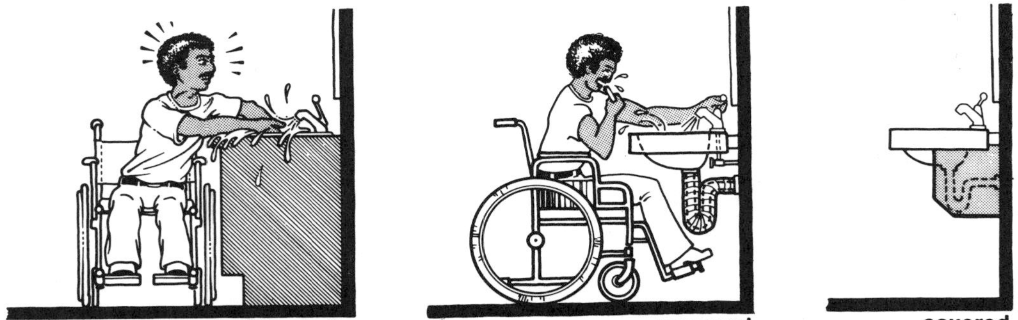

40" max.

recessed in wall

set back

covered

wrapped

inside vanity

Figure 9.
Bathrooms (continued)

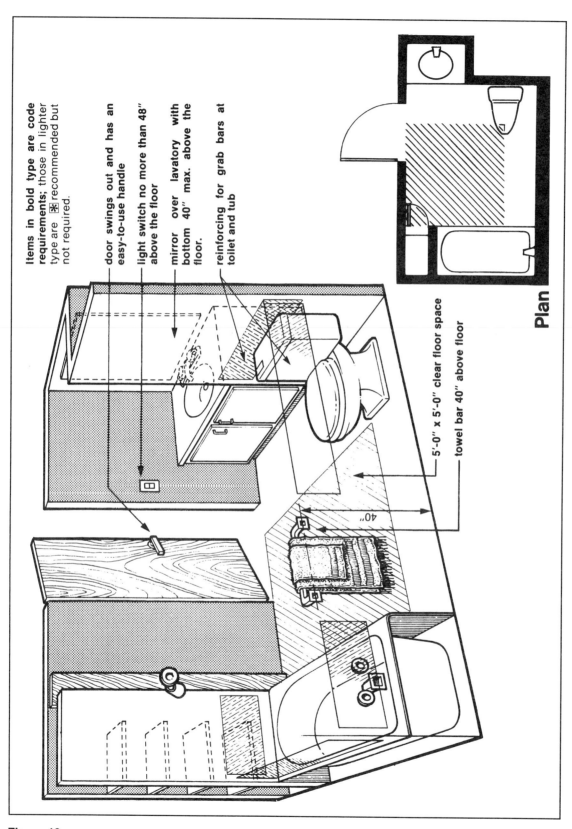

Items in bold type are code requirements; those in lighter type are ✳ recommended but not required.

door swings out and has an easy-to-use handle

light switch no more than 48" above the floor

mirror over lavatory with bottom 40" max. above the floor.

reinforcing for grab bars at toilet and tub

5'-0" x 5'-0" clear floor space

towel bar 40" above floor

40"

Plan

Figure 10.
Sample Code Complying
Bathroom

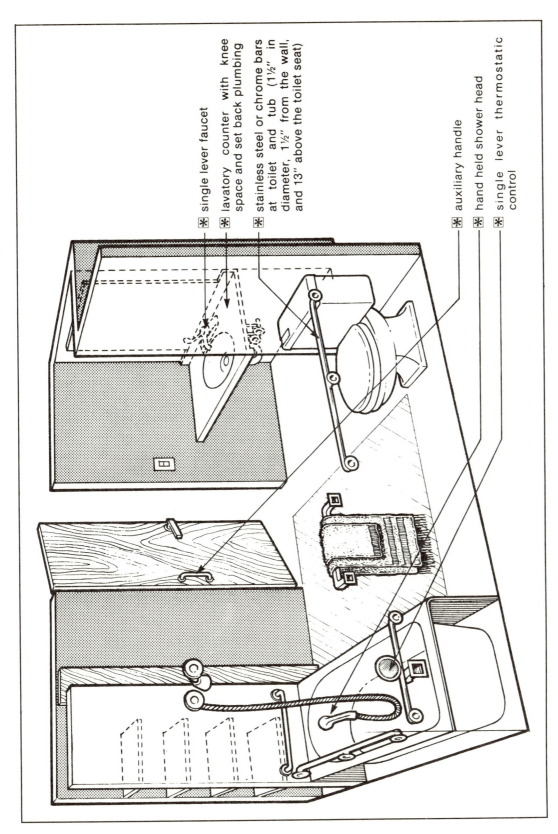

* single lever faucet

* lavatory counter with knee space and set back plumbing

* stainless steel or chrome bars at toilet and tub (1½" in diameter, 1½" from the wall, and 13" above the toilet seat)

* auxiliary handle

* hand held shower head

* single lever thermostatic control

Figure 11.
Recommended Bathroom
Features

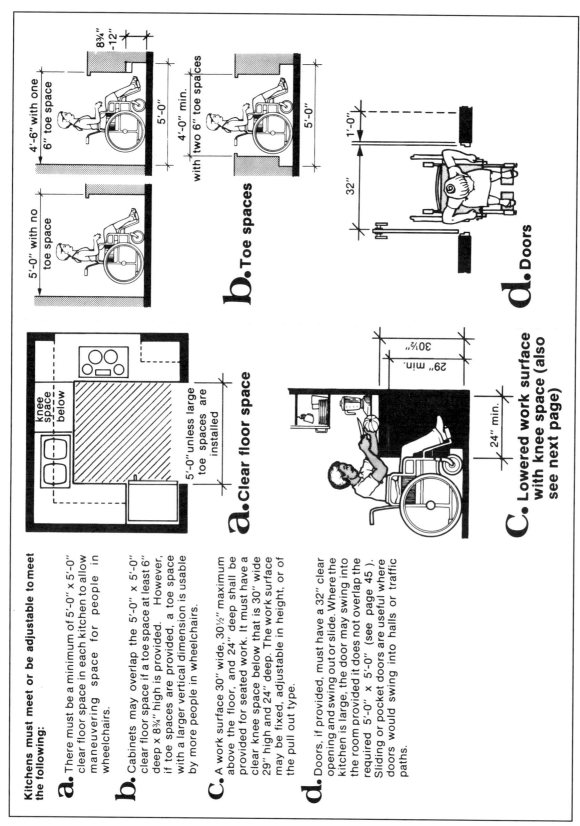

Kitchens must meet or be adjustable to meet the following:

a. There must be a minimum of 5'-0" x 5'-0" clear floor space in each kitchen to allow maneuvering space for people in wheelchairs.

b. Cabinets may overlap the 5'-0" x 5'-0" clear floor space if a toe space at least 6" deep x 8¾" high is provided. However, if toe spaces are provided, a toe space with a larger vertical dimension is usable by more people in wheelchairs.

c. A work surface 30" wide, 30½" maximum above the floor, and 24" deep shall be provided for seated work. It must have a clear knee space below that is 30" wide 29" high and 24" deep. The work surface may be fixed, adjustable in height, or of the pull out type.

d. Doors, if provided, must have a 32" clear opening and swing out or slide. Where the kitchen is large, the door may swing into the room provided it does not overlap the required 5'-0" x 5'-0" (see page 45). Sliding or pocket doors are useful where doors would swing into halls or traffic paths.

a. **Clear floor space**

b. **Toe spaces**

c. **Lowered work surface with knee space (also see next page)**

d. **Doors**

Figure 12.
Kitchens

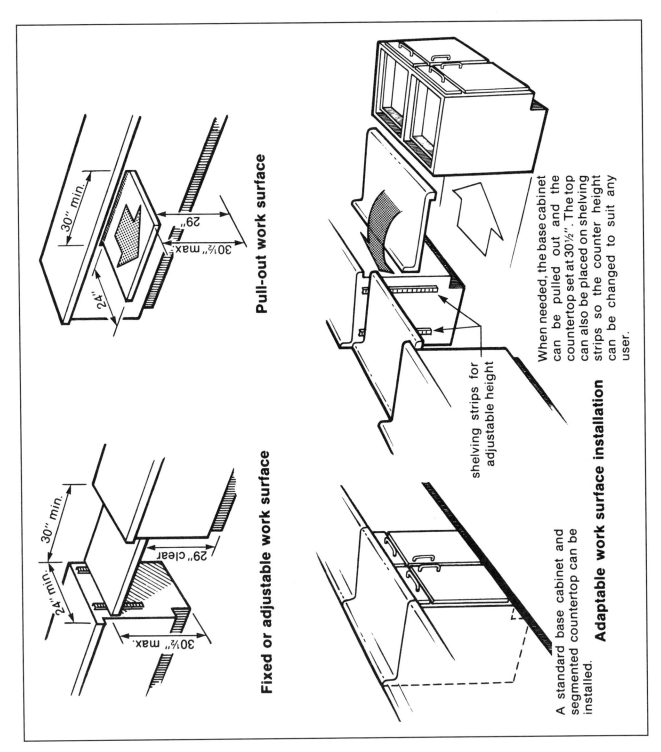

Pull-out work surface

30" min.

29"

30½" max.

24"

Fixed or adjustable work surface

30" min.

24" min.

29" clear

30½" max.

shelving strips for adjustable height

When needed, the base cabinet can be pulled out and the countertop set at 30½". The top can also be placed on shelving strips so the counter height can be changed to suit any user.

Adaptable work surface installation

A standard base cabinet and segmented countertop can be installed.

Figure 13.
Adaptable Kitchen Work
Surfaces

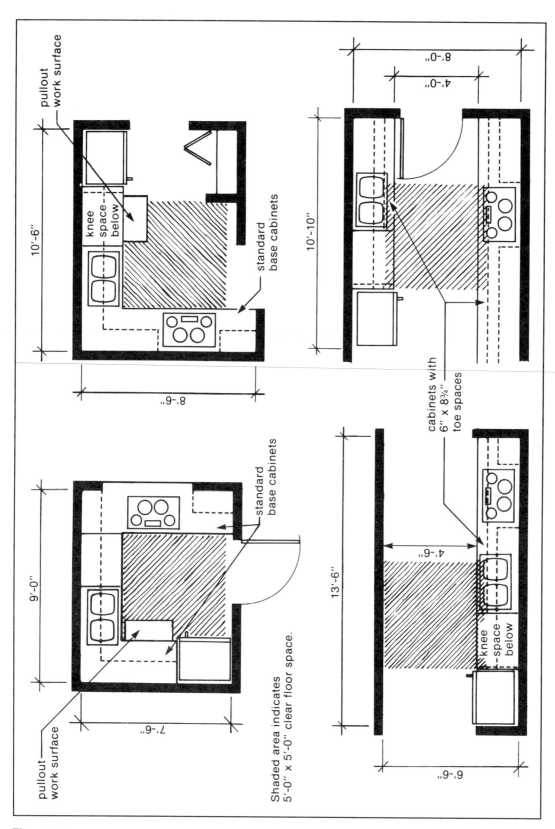

Figure 14.
Plans of Code Complying
Kitchens

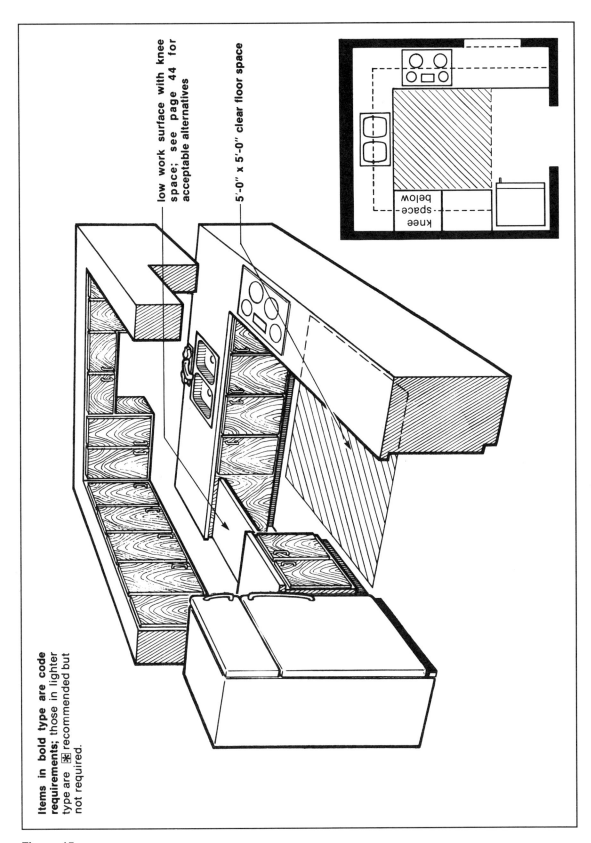

low work surface with knee space; see page 44 for acceptable alternatives

5'-0" x 5'-0" clear floor space

knee space below

Items in bold type are code requirements; those in lighter type are ✳ recommended but not required.

Figure 15.
Code Complying Kitchen

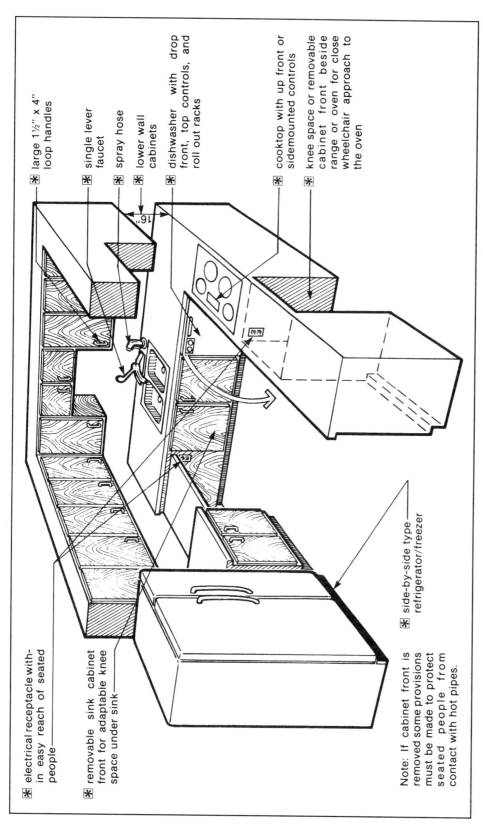

✳ large 1½" x 4" loop handles

✳ single lever faucet

✳ spray hose

✳ lower wall cabinets

✳ dishwasher with drop front, top controls, and roll out racks

✳ cooktop with up front or sidemounted controls

✳ knee space or removable cabinet front beside range or oven for close wheelchair approach to the oven

✳ electrical receptacle with- in easy reach of seated people

✳ removable sink cabinet front for adaptable knee space under sink

✳ side-by-side type refrigerator/freezer

Note: If cabinet front is removed some provisions must be made to protect seated people from contact with hot pipes.

16"

Figure 16.
Recommended Kitchen
Features

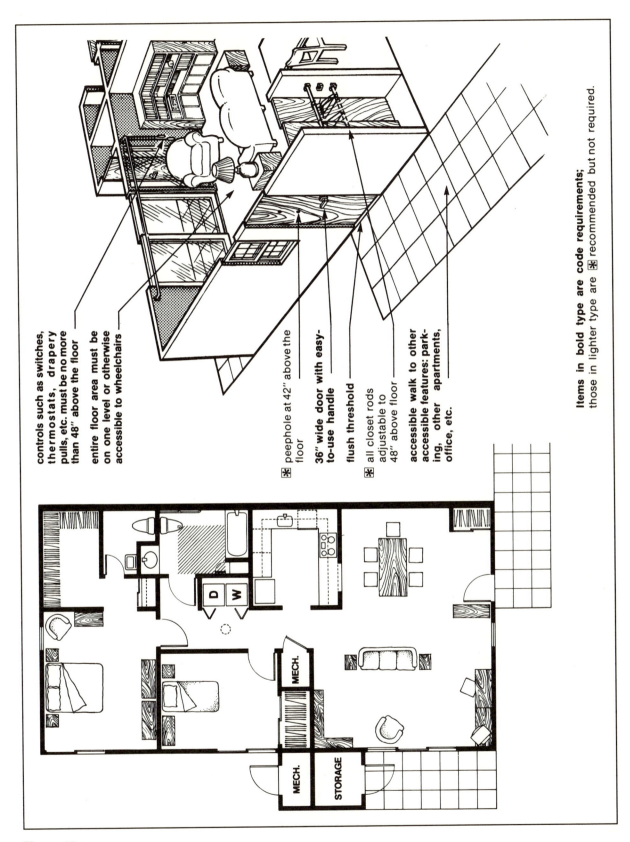

controls such as switches, thermostats, drapery pulls, etc. must be no more than 48" above the floor

entire floor area must be on one level or otherwise accessible to wheelchairs

✳ peephole at 42" above the floor

36" wide door with easy-to-use handle

flush threshold

✳ all closet rods adjustable to 48" above floor

accessible walk to other accessible features: parking, other apartments, office, etc.

Items in bold type are code requirements; those in lighter type are ✳ recommended but not required.

Figure 17.
Sample Apartment

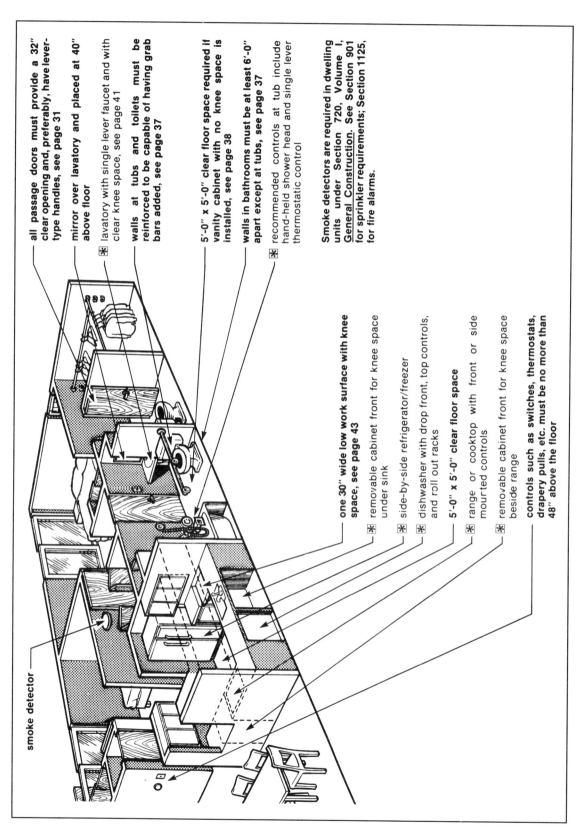

all passage doors must provide a 32" clear opening and, preferably, have lever-type handles, see page 31

mirror over lavatory and placed at 40" above floor

✳ lavatory with single lever faucet and with clear knee space, see page 41

walls at tubs and toilets must be reinforced to be capable of having grab bars added, see page 37

5'-0" x 5'-0" clear floor space required if vanity cabinet with no knee space is installed, see page 38

walls in bathrooms must be at least 6'-0" apart except at tubs, see page 37

✳ recommended controls at tub include hand-held shower head and single lever thermostatic control

Smoke detectors are required in dwelling units under Section 720, Volume I, General Construction. See Section 901 for sprinkler requirements; Section 1125, for fire alarms.

one 30" wide low work surface with knee space, see page 43

✳ removable cabinet front for knee space under sink

✳ side-by-side refrigerator/freezer

✳ dishwasher with drop front, top controls, and roll out racks

5'-0" x 5'-0" clear floor space

✳ range or cooktop with front or side mounted controls

✳ removable cabinet front for knee space beside range

controls such as switches, thermostats, drapery pulls, etc. must be no more than 48" above the floor

smoke detector

Figure 18.
Sample Apartment
(continued)

8   Finances and Asset Management

Most housing complex managers are responsible for the conduct of all tasks relative to the project's fiscal operation; among their many roles is that of asset manager. Basic financial and asset management functions for elderly housing do not materially differ from those involved in other types of housing projects; details of these operations are set forth in the IREM books listed on the final page of this volume. This chapter examines only those functions particularly characteristic of housing for the elderly. For example, it is not unusual for managers of elderly housing to assume some of the following responsibilities:

1. Assuring that each resident eligible for government or private financial assistance applies for it and receives it in good order.

2. Determining the feasibility and desirability of adding conveniences and design features such as those described in the previous chapter, to enable persons with temporary or permanent disabilities to function on a level of independence comparable to that of the able-bodied residents.

3. Creating and monitoring opportunities for residents to augment their incomes through part-time or full-time employment, such as office or maintenance work in the complex or through opportunities to market handcrafted items.

4. In the case of lifecare institutions, the task of managing the assets the resident turns over to the housing complex upon entry. Some managements require that total assets be turned over; others reserve a portion of the assets to be invested in the interests of the complex, with the rest to be invested to provide the resident with direct cash returns.

Cost Analysis

An important phase of asset management is cost analysis. For example, in a housing project—existing or proposed—that does not incorporate the special design features described in the previous chapter, the manager may need to study the feasibility of making some of these additions or improvements. In order to do so, it is necessary to determine the following:

1. The extent to which the inclusion of each additional design element raises the cost of construction or renovation and maintenance.

2. The extent to which existing financing or HUD programs can accommodate these added costs.

3. How such costs can be absorbed by the available payment mechanisms.

A sponsor can make application for housing assistance under various government programs along with the construction loan application, and may qualify for a loan at a lower interest rate from a state finance agency or from HUD or from a participating bank. Generally, the lower interest rate is made available through the sale of tax-exempt bonds. The qualified sponsor executes a regulatory document and a Housing Assistance Payment (HAP) contract along with the loan note. To apply for these loans, the sponsor should present the following:

1. Completed affirmative market plan.

2. Management plan for the community.

3. An approved management agent.

4. Management Agent qualifications folio (if HUD uses form 2530).

5. Rent-up budget (or initial budget).

6. Any other essential information, such as financial details, plans, specifications, and option to purchase for land site.

The information an asset manager needs in order to develop a cost analysis includes:

1. Documents: plans, specifications, and cost breakdown sheets.

2. Detailed quantity take-offs to account for additional design elements incorporating accessibility and adaptability (quantities of basic materials needed, plus quantities of additional materials needed for these design elements).

3. The cost of each new design element to be included (consult a cost source reference book for this information).

4. The added cost, prorated over the number of apartment units, and the cost per apartment unit.

5. Percent increases in construction costs for the respective mixes of units for the able-bodied and the disabled.

6. All sources of financing or mortgage insurance, in addition to the HUD programs in effect (to determine the implications of the additional costs).

Low-interest Subsidy Loan: An Example

Program The following example provides a basis for planning a small facility to house elderly persons, using subsidies available through the Section 202 program.

Sixteen dwelling units to be located in a single two-story masonry structure for occupancy by elderly persons and persons who are developmentally disabled. Site development will include paved driveway and parking area, landscaping and patio. The structure will include single-occupancy bedrooms, open common area, staff quarters, recreation room, and laundry facilities.

Mortgage The permanent mortgage loan will be $697,000, or 100 percent of the total development cost, whichever is less. The terms of this loan are 8.90 percent for 30 years.

Subsidy As a program, the segment of Section 8 for existing property differs fundamentally from the Section 8 segment for new construction/rehabilitation. Households participating in the Section 8 program for existing property, unlike those in Public Housing, have substantial freedom to choose their own units. A household applying and found eligible by virtue of income level and household composition may elect to stay in a unit within the administering agency's jurisdiction, if the unit meets the housing quality requirements and rent limitation, or may select another unit meeting the same criteria. Under Section 8, landlords actually receive two separate rent payments:

1. The subsidy payment from the Public Housing Agency (PHA) that administers the program;
2. The household's share, paid directly by the participating tenant.

More governmental responsibility for locating units is involved in programs such as the Section 23 program, initiated in 1965 and currently connected to Section 8. The exact basis for calculating a household's subsidy under a program such as this can have a profound effect on the extent to which elderly persons can participate.

For new construction or substantial rehabilitation, Section 8 provides a guaranteed rental stream to developers who build or renovate units under the program. The HUD area office—or sometimes a state housing finance agency—advertises the availability of funds for building or rehabilitating units in a jurisdiction; developers respond with proposals. If a proposal is found to be acceptable, HUD signs a 20- or 30-year annual contributions contract with that developer, obligating HUD to pay the difference between a tenant's rental contribution and the full rent for the unit in the project. These rents are also controlled by a separate schedule of maximum "fair market" tests for newly constructed or substantially rehabilitated units in the area. In general, the rates reflected in this schedule are higher than those used in the Section 8 "existing" segment.

The Section 202 program, created by the Housing Act of 1959, has undergone a number of changes. Currently, it provides the following:

1. The program is restricted to use by the elderly and nonelderly handicapped persons.
2. The program relies exclusively on nonprofit organizations to sponsor, develop, and operate these projects.
3. The projects, unlike the Section 8 new construction program, are financed by a direct loan to the sponsor. This relieves the sponsor of the need to seek out private financing. Section 202 projects are expected to provide more than shelter, although there are sharp limits on the health care facilities and services to be provided in each project.

Initially, the program provided loans at 0.5 percent interest above the U.S. Treasury borrowing rate. Later, it was modified to provide loans at 3 percent interest, and the sponsors were responsible for all operating expenses. Because it was felt that too many low-income households were excluded from the program because they could not afford the rentals, two changes were made in 1974:

1. The U.S. Treasury's long-term borrowing rate was adopted as the definition of the applicable interest rate.

2. A Section 8 subsidy was set aside for each unit built under the Section 202 program, to insure that at least 20 percent of the participants represented lower-income households.

Most Section 202 projects also receive some Section 8 subsidies. Overall, the Section 202 program has accounted for only a fraction of the number of units included in HUD programs, but it has been a popular one.

Developers in the program obtain mortgage financing from a private bank, from HUD through the Government National Mortgage Association (GNMA), or from a state or local agency which raises funds by selling tax-exempt bonds. HUD generally insures the mortgage through the Federal Housing Administration (FHA).

Rental Units   This housing, including utilities costs, is proposed to be subsidized under the Section 202 Housing Assistance Payments Program. In this example, the development will be totally electric, with the owner paying all utility charges. The following equipment will be provided: Range, Refrigerator/Freezer, Dishwasher/Sterilizer, Cook Top, Double Oven, Washer, Dryer, Air Conditioning, Disposal, Fire Alarm System, and Sprinkler System.

Proposed Rents   HUD limits eligibility for assistance to those who have low or very low incomes. At a minimum, 30 percent of the units are required to be reserved for persons in the very low income category. Rent is limited to 30 percent of the resident's total adjusted income.

Group Home Start-Up Budget: An Example

To help the sponsor formulate a feasible initial budget, a budget such as the example on page 89 should be prepared. In this example, a 16-unit project has one-bedroom apartments renting for an average of $328.50 per month. With an annual income of $63,072, a property tax exemption is necessary to make the project economically feasible. Utility and insurance cost estimates have been evenly divided between shelter and nonshelter costs because the dual nature of the project makes it impossible to assign the total cost to either portion of the budget.

The $4.78 per resident per day is funded through the Social Security Administration under Supplemental Security Income (SSI). This funding is an Independent Living Package to be used for room and board, or "shelter" costs. The Michigan Department of Social Services funds the $4.78 per resident per day for a social services package which provides salaries for staffing the home with individuals able to assist the residents in attaining the highest possible level of self-sufficiency and employability. It also provides for any services which enhance the in-house programming of the home.

Project Cost Estimates: An Example

In order to estimate what extra construction costs, if any, might be incurred by incorporating the design elements that would promote independent living on the part of disabled residents, it is sometimes desirable to examine multifamily projects that are in the process of construction or renovation. The following is

Group Home Start-Up Budget

Shelter Costs	Annual	Per Diem
Maintenance/Repair	$ 2,000	$ .34
Utilities* (Gas, Electricity, Water and Sewer)	1,700	.29
Debt Service	16,000	2.74
Reserves	1,200	.21
Property Taxes	0	.00
Insurance*	400	.07
Food and Supplies	12,295	2.11
Vacancy (2.5 percent)	1,182	.025
	$ 34,777	$ 5.95

Nonshelter Costs	Annual	Per Diem
Manager and Relief	$ 9,500	$ 1.63
Operating Personnel	4,500	.77
Administrative Expense	4,500	.77
Payroll Taxes (15 percent)	2,400	.41
Utilities*	1,700	.29
Insurance*	400	.07
Legal and Audit	400	.07
Supplies	500	.09
Transportation (Other than to work)	4,000	.68
	$27,900	4.78
TOTAL EXPENSES	$62,677	$10.73

an example of the cost considerations involved in the construction of a complex of apartments and townhouses in San Diego, California. Some of the design elements involved no extra cost because they were included in the original plans. Some actually resulted in net savings rather than added cost.

The project includes 100 dwelling units in 6 two-story townhouse buildings and 4 two-story apartment buildings. The townhouse buildings contain 20 three-bedroom units and 16 four-bedroom units. The apartment buildings contain 8 three-bedroom units and 56 two-bedroom units. In addition, the complex contains a small—1,400 square foot—community building. Cost of the project is estimated to be $2,166,550. That is about $21.60 per square foot. For the average dwelling unit, that amounts to $21,666.

Barrier-Free Circulation   To make *site access* completely barrier-free, only curb cuts are needed. Additional cost is negligible because little additional forming or finishing work is required. The cost is about $300.

Original plans for *access to each of the 36 townhouses* called for a one-step stoop, four feet wide. Substituting a four-foot-wide ramp for the stoop can, in addition to providing for wheelchair access, effect net *savings* of $641.

36 stoops, 4'x4', @ $8.85 per square foot, would cost $1,275.

36 ramps, 4'x4', @ $1.10 per square foot, would cost   634.

$ 641.

Access to each of the 8 apartment buildings originally called for a one-step stoop; substituting a ramp, with all dimensions and costs as for the townhouses, *saves* $144.

Raised numbers to aid the blind cost $30 each for a set of four. This amounts to $1,080 for the apartments and $14,480 for the townhouses. *Automatic door openers* for the convenience of those using wheelchairs or walkers, and carrying packages, cost $1,515 each; for eight locations, that would be $12,200. *Replacing doorknobs with levers* at 328 locations adds up to $2,624. No extra cost is involved in replacing knobs or recessed pulls with ring-type handles. Installation of elevators in two-story buildings would not be recommended. Instead, the plan calls for availability of second-floor dwelling-units to be limited to those whose disabilities do not preclude their climbing stairs. Replacing dwelling-unit doorknockers, @ $15 each, with *doorbells* @ $105, results in a net cost of $3,240 for the townhouses and $6,660 for the apartments. Because the original plans include prewiring of these dwelling-units on a low-voltage system that accommodates the installation of special signals such as a flashing light for the deaf or an odor-introducing device for the deaf-blind, no additional wiring costs are incurred in adapting each system for the particular needs of the resident who is to use it. *Widening doors to 36 inches for wheelchair passage* needs to be done only for first-floor apartments, because second-floor residents can climb stairs. The cost of widening 136 doors at $10 each is $1,360.

Emergency Communication System All 36 townhouse units should be included in the emergency communication system. This involves a single-call station, with speaker and microphone for each dwelling-unit, at $200, and a master control panel to monitor calls, at about $90 per unit. In toto, this calls for $10,800 for the townhouses, and $19,200 for the apartments. As new residents introduce needs that have not yet been accommodated, new features can be added. Fire alarms, for instance, must be designed with visual warnings for the deaf, and with odor dispensers or high-powered fans for the deaf/blind. However, the costs of these features need not be reflected in the initial cost estimates.

Floors Replacing carpeting, at $10.25 per square yard, or a total of $37,000, with smooth, nonslip flooring, such as vinyl asbestos tiles, at .89 per square foot, or $28,925, yields a net *savings* of $8,000.

Bathrooms and Kitchens Installing electrical outlets and switches in appropriate locations at heights that are conveniently within reach incurs no extra cost. If the building code permits, vinyl tubing, flexible metal tubing, or similar materials, can be used as supply piping. ABS or similar plastic can be used for waste piping, and longer or shorter pieces added as necessary. Unless cast iron and copper, involving labor costs, must be used, this should involve only conventional costs. The cost of accessories such as extra grab bar reinforcing, 18-inch-high toilets, and tubside transfer seating, would be about $50. For the number of bathrooms estimated to need these changes, the total should come to about $2,000. Adding 30 square feet, at $21.60 per square foot, to each of the 36 ground-floor bathrooms, costs $23,328. This changes the bathroom dimensions from 7'x5' to 10'x6'6".

The cost of adaptation for the kitchen is difficult to estimate because there has been little precedent for this practice. All first-floor kitchen sinks should have flexible plumbing as described in the previous paragraph in order to raise or lower countertops within a range of 38 to 36 inches from the floor. Hardware and fasteners are needed for the raising and lowering process. The undersink cabinet should be removable.

Summary of Added Costs

Emergency Communication System	$ 30,000
Doorbell System for res. mgr. apt.	240
Ramps	(144)
Automatic Door Opener at main entry	12,200
Wider Doors*	1,360
Increase bathrooms 30 sq. ft.*	23,300
Replace knobs with door levers	2,624
Replace knobs/recessed pulls with ring-type handles	0
Replace carpet with vinyl tile*	(8,000)
Adaptable kitchen cabinetry*	1,880
Adapted bathrooms*	2,000
Switches and outlets at proper levels	0
Site access	300
Community facility	1,250
Total additional cost	76,450
Total additional cost adjusted	81,600
*Total original estimate***	$2,166,550
Total new estimate	$2,248,150

Unit Cost Summary

Total added for 64 apartments	60,720
This includes:	
Ramps	(144)
Emergency Communication System	19,200
Doorbell System	5,766
Raised Numbers (at 8 locations)	240
Total added cost per apartment:	
First Floor	1,458
Second Floor	440
Total added for 36 townhouses:	$ 14,480
This includes:	
Ramps	(640)
Emergency Communication System	10,800
Doorbell System	3,240
Raised Numbers	1,080
Total added cost per townhouse	$ 402

Figures in parentheses represent deductions.

Percent increase is 3.75 over original estimate, based on the addition of the design elements as described in the foregoing portion of this chapter.

*Added or deducted costs apply only to 32 first-floor apartments.

**Original estimate is current as of 1983.

The case illustrated is fictional, although it is based on actual cost figures for units similar to those described here. It is intended as an example only.

Financial Management: Residents

The three main areas of management services, tasks, and functions relating to residents of housing for the elderly are rent collection, budget preparation, and accounting/cost control. Additional services include monitoring sources of possible income and benefits to residents, and sources of opportunities for employment and volunteer work. The manager can also provide information on financial management and consumer advocacy groups and programs. In these respects, management of housing for disabled elderly residents does not differ markedly from that of those who are able-bodied. All these functions and services can be performed by the assistant manager in lieu of, or in addition to, the manager.

Rent Collection

The manager physically and personally collects rent payments, or receives them from tenants who choose to drop them off at the office, and credits them to the proper individuals. In the event of delinquency, the manager visits the resident to discuss payment of arrears. If there are unusual financial problems, a management meeting, or hearing, can be held to determine the best course of action.

Budget Preparation

The budget is prepared by the manager, who, in some cases, has staff assistance. The manager presents the figures to the ownership or governing board of the project for approval. The procedures are the same, of course, whether or not any of the residents are disabled. Special guidelines apply to the handling of subsidies and other governmental assistance.

Accounting/Cost Control

Only in the larger projects is a professional accountant is needed to handle the accounting and cost control functions. For most elderly housing projects, the manager or assistant can take care of these procedures:

1. Posting of income; bank deposits.
2. Payment of bills under limits authorized by a governing board. Vouchering of bills above those limits, for authorization by the board.
3. Accounting functions.
4. Reporting periodically to a governing board on the status of accounts and the financial position of the project.

Income Sources for Residents

One of the manager's invaluable services is to make residents aware of benefits to which they are entitled, and to make sure those benefits are received by the proper individuals. The importance of such benefits is emphasized by the percentage of the total income of elderly persons represented by the following categories:

Source	Percentages
Social Security	26
Retirement Funds, Insurance, Private Investment	29
Other Assistance, e.g., Public Welfare	45

Management should circulate information on all possible benefits, including directions on how and where to apply for them. For instance, a resident may be eligible for unemployment insurance benefits; the manager can give the resident any help needed in order to file a claim with the state employment service. Newsletters and bulletin boards are good media to use for this purpose, and question-and-answer sessions on new developments are helpful.

Sources of Information on Benefits

Management can serve as coordinator among national agencies such as Social Security and the Veterans Administration (VA), and also among local assistance programs, obtaining the necessary information for the residents and providing the agencies with basic data from the tenants' files. The Social Security Administration has local offices containing data on all Social Security programs such as Old Age Survivors (Medicare) programs. Payments are based largely on employment history. A booklet, *Social Security Programs in the U.S.A.*, is available from the Superintendent of Documents at the Government Printing Office in Washington, D.C. The address is listed in Appendix B of this book.

The Veterans Administration provides assistance for persons who have served in the armed forces of the United States, for their families, and for their survivors. The Bibliography lists the source of a booklet explaining availability of these benefits. Help with questions relating to Veterans Administration benefits may also be obtained from the local VA office, where counselors can render advice on specific cases.

To resolve questions relating to retirement concerns such as pensions, other income programs, and taxation, it may be advisable to contact the local Legal Aid Society. To answer legal questions of a general nature, some communities have established a hotline telephone service that plays recorded messages on a wide variety of subjects.

Some communities have information and referral services. Most larger communities publish a directory listing them. Copies should be made available to the residents of the elderly housing complex. In most areas, one department of local government maintains responsibility for administering the various public assistance programs, including Old Age Assistance and Medicaid. This department may be designated as Human Resources, Public Assistance or Welfare. Representatives of the department, or other individuals knowledgeable in this area, can be invited to tenant organization meetings to give talks or just answer questions about availability of benefits.

The public library is another good source of information. If the housing complex has its own small library, it might be possible to subscribe to publications monitoring changes in benefit programs; some are issued by the government; others by associations distributing information of interest to the elderly population. These associations are listed in Appendixes A and B.

A group of residents can be trained to serve as a referral center for their fellow residents. They can aid in distributing materials and in following up individual cases to see that applicants actually receive aid. They may also be helpful in that some residents may prefer to discuss these benefit programs with another resident rather than with someone representing the project management.

Retirement Careers

Opportunities for employment may exist within the housing complex. In some projects, residents are employed to handle the switchboard and other office tasks, maintenance work, security services, housekeeping, and bookkeeping. Retired teachers, artists, industrial workers, and other specialists conduct classes on a variety of subjects for residents. Some managers prefer to pay compensation directly; others prefer to deduct the earned amount from the rent each month. In some projects, residents can rent space on the ground floor to conduct small businesses, such as craft and gift shops, and locksmith services.

Retired workers who have acquired skills and proficiency as hobbyists may choose to develop a part-time activity into a retirement career. Others may wish to resume use of their career skills and knowledge, or learn what is needed to enter a new field of endeavor. The U.S. Department of Labor has

HUD

The manager can help the resident who desires part-time or full-time employment by establishing contact with reputable agencies.

published a booklet, *Back to Work After Retirement*, available from the Superintendent of Documents at the Government Printing Office. The complete address is listed in Appendix B of this book.

The manager can help the resident who desires full-time or part-time employment by establishing contact with a number of agencies. The state employment service, for example, provides information about jobs that are available, interviews applicants, and refers them to potential employers. State and local employment agencies, and the U.S. Department of Labor conduct manpower development programs available to elderly persons. Work incentive programs for skilled and unskilled workers are conducted by many local welfare departments. Programs to help disabled persons achieve the highest possible degree of independence are conducted by state vocational rehabilitation agencies. "Senior Aids," funded by the U.S. Department of Labor, employs low-income citizens who are 55 and older at federal minimum wage 20 hours per week in child care centers, adult education programs, and other community services. Detailed information on these programs can be obtained from the National Council of Senior Citizens and the American Association of Retired Persons. "Senior Opportunities and Services (S.O.S.)" is a program focusing on opportunities for employment and volunteer work for persons 55 and older. A contract with the National Council on Aging and Project FIND provides employment. Further information can be obtained by writing to the Community Action Program, Office of Human Development Services, and to the National Council on the Aging.

Redesign of jobs to create opportunities for employment of elderly persons is a relatively easy matter, and it helps employers make use of practised skills rather than to invest the time and money to train someone who is new to the field. The manager of a housing complex for the elderly may be able to interest local businesses in instituting such programs where they are not already in place. Job-sharing also is feasible for some who wish to work a limited number of hours a day or week.

Adult education programs are available in local colleges, junior colleges, and high schools, to prepare workers for new types of employment, and for new types of technology in many fields. Computer science classes, for example, are available in a large number of communities. Many offer lowered tuition rates to senior citizens.

Helping Residents Stretch Their Dollars

Tax Relief for the Project   An opportunity for direct monetary savings for the elderly resident can result from the savings afforded the project management by ad valorem tax exemptions. The manager who applies for this tax relief for the project, and receives it, benefits not only the project but all of its residents as well, by passing on these savings in the form of significant reductions in monthly rent.

In-House Thrift Shop   With the guidance and cooperation of management, residents can organize and run a thrift shop on the premises. This provides an opportunity for residents to sell used clothing and other articles, and any handicrafts they produce. It provides employment for those who are active in running it. For all the residents, it offers convenient access to shopping for desired goods at affordable prices. Residents who have had experience in purchasing or retail sales might form the nucleus of a group that gets the shop going, and then provides training for other residents who want to participate in the business. Some basic policies should be established before the grand opening, dealing with questions such as whether the shop should be opened to the public or to project residents only, what security measures are to be taken, business days and hours, what (if any) profit margin should be set, and how profits and staff compensation should be administered. The system need not be complex. Even simple barter, within a limited framework, can work well if all participants understand and agree with the terms. Whatever ground rules are chosen, it is important to put them in writing and make them available to each resident in the complex. As changes are made, updated information should be circulated. As shop activity increases, it may provide funds for other projects.

Cooperative Shopping   Because "the large economy size" of most grocery and drugstore items is not economical when purchased for one or two persons who have little storage space, most residents of housing for the elderly can gain some financial advantage by pooling shopping lists with neighbors on a regular basis. If this opportunity is offered to all the residents of the complex, it becomes possible to make the purchases at volume prices, and receive appropriate quantities at considerable savings—not only savings in initial cost, but avoidance of the waste that results from futile attempts to utilize too large a supply. The date and time shopping lists should be turned in in order to participate in this service should be posted on bulletin boards, and included in the newsletter or fact sheet each resident receives. The entire order should be delivered to one established location in the complex, for pickup by the individual residents. A limited in-house delivery service can be made available

HUD

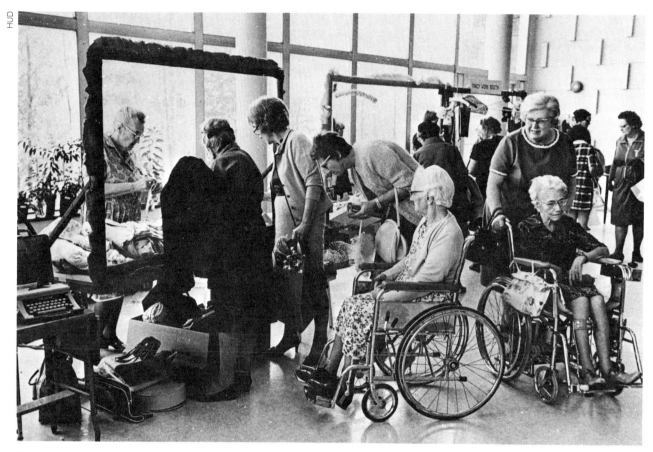

*Residents can organize and
run a thrift shop on the
premises.*

to those who through disability, illness or absence cannot themselves convey
the goods to their apartments at delivery time.

Discounts Arrangements for discounts for elderly persons can be made with
local stores and restaurants. A discount card might be devised for this purpose,
on agreement with the residents to make the effort to patronize these places.
College and high school student government groups that have worked out such
arrangements can help provide guidance as to how these agreements are
drawn up. Once the discount cards are distributed, reminders encouraging
their use should be given to the residents periodically.

Discounts can also be obtained on request from beauty shops, barber shops,
and other services desired by the residents. Movie and theatre discounts might
come in the form of tickets for special performances, or "two-fers" (two tickets
for the price of one). Taxicab companies sometimes offer a senior citizen rate,
or book of low-cost tickets. Banks in many areas offer elderly persons an
exemption from the checking account service charge—similar to the
exemption they offer to students.

Consumer Advocacy Projects Hearing impairment is one example of an
affliction of some elderly persons that can result in their exploitation by
unscrupulous vendors. Misunderstanding of what is being told or sold to them
may well eventually cost more than the victim contemplated bargaining for.

The manager can help protect residents from these situations, and can provide guidance to the wise use of income. Consumer education, consumer protection, and legal aid can help elderly persons with regard to shopping, budget planning, and awareness of consumer rights. Further information can be obtained by writing to the organizations listed in Appendixes A and B.

9   The Future of Housing for the Elderly

The Growing Demand

A growth curve representing the demand for managers of housing for the elderly would clearly arch upward sharply in the 1980s and 90s, leveling off only in the third decade of the next century. Essential to this specialty are the psychosocial insights and professional property management techniques discussed in the foregoing chapters of this book. Another essential is the subject of this final chapter: the ability to recognize and monitor trends that shape the future needs elderly housing is to serve. Preparation to make decisions that accommodate tenants' needs as they change over time, in the ways that best utilize available materials, services, and community assistance, requires ongoing attention to the changing nature of the elderly population, and the ability to develop appropriate resources and opportunities.

The Future Elderly

The increases in the human lifespan that have been noted over the past several decades are expected to continue throughout the next fifty years, and perhaps for a time beyond. Research has indicated to some gerontologists and geriatrists that this trend will probably level off when the average "natural" lifespan has reached about 100 years. This carries a number of implications for the planning of new construction and the renovation of existing buildings, the most obvious of which is that there will be much greater numbers of elderly persons to be housed.

Slowing the Aging Process

Increasing the number of years it takes to reach the limits of the average lifespan also stretches the number of years in each of life's stages: longer old age means longer youth, adolescence, maturity, and middle age. This would not automatically be true; it would be possible to prolong the "old-old" stage through life-support systems without dramatically improving the quality and length of each stage of life—but medical research reports indicate that the success of efforts to combat acute illnesses in each age bracket does indicate improvement throughout the lengthened lifespan. Misdiagnosis has been a problem for the elderly. Research on Alzheimer's disease, long considered the most common cause of severe intellectual impairment in older persons, has revealed that, while the cause of this neurological ailment is still being studied, a large percentage of persons diagnosed as having the disease have actually been suffering from nutritional deficiencies, thyroid disease, improper medication, or clinical depression—all potentially treatable conditions if detected in an early stage. Elderly persons formerly were thought to be "too set in their ways" to benefit from treatment of clinical depression; now, the American Psychological Association reports excellent results from such treatment.

They are typically motivated for treatment . . . and we have found that older adults progress in therapy at least as rapidly as do their younger cohorts . . . Moreover, because older patients are "more in touch with their own mortality," they often work harder to succeed in this type of treatment (Report of National Institute of Mental Health conference on the psychodynamic treatment of older persons, *APA Monitor* 14, no. 8 [August 1983]).

With these advances in coping with the problems of acute illnesses and depression comes the prospect of opportunities to concentrate research efforts on the chronic illnesses and debility of the "old-old" years—another indication of the potential to improve health and strength for those who reach that stage in the future.

This is particularly meaningful in terms of perception of one's own prospects. Self-perception as "middle-aged" rather than "old" at 70, for example, can stimulate the vigor, optimism, and independence to continue to be physically and socially active, and avoid much of the depression and discouragement that in the past have caused many in the retirement years to undergo the process of disengagement. The planning process should include the following considerations:

1. Those who are physically but not financially independent at minimum retirement age will experience an urgent need for low-cost housing that incorporates security and safety features.
2. Length of tenant occupancy will increase.
3. Those persons who are physically and financially independent in their 60s, 70s, and early 80s, will generally remain "in place"—entering retirement housing only at or beyond their late 80s. At that point, they will probably seek housing that incorporates some of the supportive features that are shown in chapter 7.

Increasing Numbers of "Old-Old"

Because the "old-old" are the fastest-growing segment of the population, and because of the prospect of increase in length of tenant occupancy, the manager of an elderly housing complex in the future may well find that the change in age mix will create a different social atmosphere, along with an increase in need for services and supportive design features. The social program in the complex can help maintain an even emphasis on ages and stages by taking care to present programs and events in sufficient variety to meet each group's expectations. Sensitivity to needs for services—even those the tenant does not request—will be important.

Increasing Variety of Tastes and Lifestyles

Research on family life in 1900 revealed that the lifestyles of middle-aged persons were indistinguishable from the lifestyles of the elderly—a natural result of the narrow (47-year) average lifespan. Increasing the number of years involved in each stage of the aging process has resulted in a multigenerational group designated as "elderly" or "old" that is notable for its heterogeneity of tastes and lifestyles. Housing facilities designed for this group must be versatile enough to accommodate both the "young-old" son or daughter and that tenant's "old-old" parent. In future years, the parent may move into an "older-old" category, as the "young-old" person becomes "old-old," and a grandchild reaches "young-old" status. It is important to recognize that this is a population that differs in its perspectives on retirement living. Most of those in the oldest group grew up with the idea of the retirement years as a time of rest and quiet relaxation after a lifetime of striving to meet occupational goals. Succeeding generations have been active in seeking political and social changes; retirement from careers may free more of their time to devote to these issues. Many who enter retirement housing may pursue part-time or full-time careers, on or off the premises. Flexibility and adaptability in communications and social programs will be needed more and more as time goes on in order to meet the needs of persons so diverse in backgrounds, goals and values. For example, bilingual communication has already become necessary in many areas. The manager should be aware of individuals' preferences, so that the diffident person who really wishes to participate in group activities is sufficiently encouraged to do so, and, at the same time, the resident who wishes time to be alone can be notified of activities and events without feeling pushed into them. Of course, these statements also apply to current housing for the elderly, but their importance will grow with the increase in variety and numbers of these tenants.

The shortage of housing for the elderly does not mean that all units are automatically leased as soon as they become available. On the contrary, vacancies exist in projects only a few blocks from complexes with lengthy waiting lists. The reason is simply that in order to serve the elderly population, housing must meet all the needs involved—physical, social and financial. The shortage of such housing in the United States, and the prospect of meeting their needs where the cost of living might be lower have led pensioners to invest their savings in relocation to housing offered in other countries. Israel, Spain, and the Scandinavian countries have attracted many. The Association of Americans and Canadians in Israel, Senior Branch, has acted to remedy Israel's shortage of elderly housing.

From the project's inception, investors in the nonprofit co-operative have been actively involved in every stage of planning and construction. They studied retirement communities in Europe and America, and hired an American "programming company" to fit the best of everything into their design. They personally selected architects and engineers, and brought energy conservationists and environmental psychologists out from the United States. . . . The site was chosen not only for its magnificent view, but also for its proximity to bus routes, shopping, community centers and two major hospitals. . . . All apartments—1½, 2 and 2½ unfurnished rooms—are compact and accessible. . . . Doors are wide enough for wheelchairs and bathtubs or shower stalls are equipped with hand grips . . . electric ovens are fitted with a reminder light, and all rooms, including bathrooms, feature emergency intercom buttons connected to the reception desk. A 24-hour security guard and qualified nurse will be automatically alerted if a telephone is disconnected. Lights are fitted beneath the kitchen cupboards for those whose sight is failing (*The Israel Economist* [August 1983], p. 37).

The complex includes a health-care unit, an infirmary, a central dining room, a library, hobby and game rooms, a self-service laundry, a beauty parlor, and an underground parking garage.

Changing Physical Needs

Planning housing needs involves a process of envisioning today's tenants as they will be 10, 15, and 20 years from now—for example, the abilities and needs of today's 62-year-olds at 72, 77, and 82, and those of today's 82-year-olds at 92, 97, and 102. It is anticipated that future residents will enter their retirement years healthier and more physically active than preceding generations were at that point in their lives. In addition to providing sufficient interior space for meetings and other gatherings, it will be more important than ever to provide protected outdoor areas for some sports activities as well as for resting and relaxation. For instance, persons who have taken up jogging in their earlier years will wish to continue with it—and will be well advised to do so. Usage of sports equipment and facilities should be made conditional initially upon a physician's recommendation and subsequently upon the reports of periodic checkups or monitoring of basic health indicators. Each resident should be helped to realize the importance of regular checkups, and of prompt attention to major and minor physical changes, for early detection and treatment of ailments.

The National Center for Housing Management suggests making health care conveniently accessible by providing space for a community health service agency on the premises—either rent-free or at a limited rent. The same arrangement could be made with a private clinic or group of doctors. The ready availability of such outpatient and emergency services can play an important part in maintaining the health and relative physical independence of the residents. The effort to help the resident maintain the greatest possible degree of independence not only reflects a compassionate attitude on the part of management but also reflects a financial verity:

Dependence is costly to the individuals, their families, and to the public (*Housing for a Maturing Population* [Washington, D.C.: Urban Land Institute, 1983], p. 53).

If, as a result of a checkup or trauma, it becomes evident that a resident needs one or more supportive features such as those described in chapter 7 in order to continue occupying the dwelling-unit, the cost of that housing will rise. If there is no clear policy on this question, the manager may need to take up with the owner the advisability of installing the needed features. If they are not made available, and the tenant must seek other housing, the cost of a vacancy is incurred; eventually, the elderly tenant who moves into that space may be faced with a similar situation. The foregoing chapters have shown that incorporating supportive features into the planning and design of an elderly housing project as a whole can be cost-effective as a means of promoting stable occupancy. These features also attract new tenants who hope to occupy their dwelling units on a long-term basis. Tenants who do not need such features generally regard them as conveniences they are glad to have included in their units. As a whole, they value features such as the placement of electrical outlets within convenient reach rather than the usual just-above-baseboard location.

Lifecare facilities, as previous chapters have pointed out, customarily provide whatever health care is needed, typically on the premises. The following changes are predicted for the future:

1. The "virtually unlimited" health care benefits now provided for residents will become an "unaffordable burden to the facilities." Newer facilities of

Mitzit

Incorporating supportive features, such as these wooden hand rails, in elderly housing can be cost-effective.

this type will place some limits on the amount of health care provided; residents will need to seek some form of health insurance to provide the rest.

2. Nursing home benefits and needs not covered by Medicare or existing insurance contracts will be addressed by major insurance companies through new forms of coverage.

3. Regulations to "monitor the development and operation of lifecare/ continuing-care communities" have been enacted in several states, and will be enacted in others, to "provide useful protection for residents without strangling development of future communities."

4. Sources of funds for Medicaid, welfare, food stamps, and similar programs might be used to fund lifecare communities, at "little or no increase in overall cost to taxpayers." Funding for proprietary lifecare communities might come from investors using the property as a source of depreciation benefits—and, upon exhaustion of those benefits, a source of potential capital gains through resale of the property.

5. A refundable entry fee for residents would provide the capital to develop a lifecare facility, and the resulting lower interest and debt service charges would lower the operating costs (*Laventhol & Horwath 1983 Survey*).

A report from Laventhol & Horwath also suggests that "apartment building owners consider converting property into continuing-care retirement centers if faced with low rentals and little hope of selling or converting to condominiums."

Changing Nonshelter Service Needs

The most commonly cited reason for applying for elderly housing is that the applicant is having difficulty with the chores involved in home maintenance. With only the housekeeping for the dwelling-unit in the housing complex to do, the tenant can usually function independently for the first years of occupancy. If strength and energy wane, and illness occurs later, housekeeping services usually are sought on an individual basis; a list of sources is provided by the manager. As a large proportion of residents moves into the "old-old" category, and service needs increase, the manager of an "independent living" complex may find it practical to offer several service options, ranging from light to heavy work, and from weekly to daily, through a subcontracting arrangement with a commercial service. In congregate housing, and "supported-living" facilities, such as nursing homes, housekeeping services, and linen services, are included in the housing agreement with the resident.

The movement of large numbers of "young-old" into housing for the elderly within the next several decades will introduce new levels of physical self-reliance and social interaction into the retirement community. Financial need and desire for environmental protection will be their prime motivation for applying for this housing. Once established, this group of future elderly are expected to desire an active role in self-management, and organization of social, educational, and recreational programs. Their efforts, well channeled by the manager, can accomplish many of the tasks that the manager formerly had to call upon staff members or community volunteers to do: for example, the formation of committees to prepare for special events, recruitment of teams to provide assistance to others in cases of emergency, and the use of occupational or leisure-time talents to teach crafts and skills to others. Residents who are active within the retirement community often can succeed in drawing in a fellow resident's family members to become participants in community events, and relate more closely to that resident rather than to remain passive, occasional visitors.

An example of tenant initiative and sensitivity to the needs of elderly persons is recounted in the August, 1983, issue of *The Israel Economist*. A couple had planned a five-figure bequest to establish a fund to fill special needs not met by other funds available to the elderly—that something extra that can make the difference between merely "existing" and "living." Widowed in her mid-70s, the surviving spouse decided to wait no longer to make the fund available. Examples of needs being served are: a radio, a subscription to a newspaper in the native language of a lonely immigrant, concert tickets for a music lover living on a small pension, dental and post-operative care not covered by insurance, curtains for a window. In each case, wise and thoughtful use of a small amount of money has made a great difference in a tenant's outlook on life.

Of course, the manager must monitor such efforts in keeping with the policies that have been established for the complex, but the future elderly, representing the healthiest, best-educated generation in history, are expected to have the ability and the motivation to take on the responsibility for a number of their own social services. This will probably not be accomplished without an occasional difference of opinion, or even a clash of wills, but, in general, it should promote a vigorous program of activity that should function to the satisfaction and benefit of the community as a whole.

HUD

Residents can use companies' training and equipment at home in "cottage industry" employment.

Changing Career Options

The exigencies of retirement on a reduced income in a volatile economy have created hardships for many persons who must struggle to meet their obligations, and have little opportunity to expand their resources. For some persons, this has meant a necessity to seek some form of employment— part-time or full-time—to reach even a minimal standard of living. For most of those in good health who can find or continue with employment, this has worked out to be an aid to maintaining morale and a feeling of self-worth. Most of those who have responded to survey questions have expressed a wish for such an opportunity. In periods of widespread unemployment, persons in the retirement years compete with those in the prime of life for even the least desirable positions. However, the trend of previous decades toward early retirement has been reversed, and there is new encouragement for workers to remain active in their fields of endeavor. Although for many this is not possible, because of a shift in the economy or technology, some new employment options are anticipated. Previous chapters have mentioned opportunities within the housing complex, such as maintenance or office work, or pursuit of a craft, skill, or service in a retail outlet on the premises. Local chapters of national organizations devoted to the interests of the elderly have worked to promote job opportunities for the elderly within those communities. The Senior Community Service Employment Program (SCSEP), authorized under Title V of the Older Americans Act, supports more than 50,000 part-time jobs for older, low-income men and women. The development of electronic technology has already provided many persons with "cottage industry" types of employment. For example, large banks install computers and word processors in the homes of part-time or full-time employees who can then perform clerical or communications functions on a regular basis. This equipment, installed within a housing complex for the elderly, can, and undoubtedly will provide employment for many residents. Retraining of individuals to qualify them for these and other types of employment will be held on the premises of housing complexes, or arrangements made for transporting resident trainees to sessions presented at the company sites.

Future Housing Trends

There is a trend away from the planning of elderly housing for the exclusive occupancy of able-bodied persons. Legislative protection of the rights of disabled persons through the provisions of the Uniform Barrier-Free Act requires that all public buildings be made accessible to them, and that a standard percentage of the units in public housing be equipped with the features that these residents need in order to maintain their ability to live independently. These efforts began decades ago, with the frustrations of public housing managers who had to cope with the temporary illnesses and disabilities of residents in housing designed for independent living. These residents' needs could not be accommodated within public housing policies and procedures. Instead, the managers installed the needed adaptive features wherever feasible to do so without incurring censure by government inspectors. Many managers in the public and private sectors believe that the flexibility of congregate housing is the wave of the future for the housing of the elderly. Accessibility of supportive features and services—particularly health services—becomes more important with the passing years. Emergency treatment centers and clinics have been constructed adjacent to elderly housing facilities. Retirement housing is being built on the grounds of hospitals and nursing homes. The grounds of large universities are also considered desirable sites for new or converted housing complexes for the elderly.

The growth of the elderly population—approximately five percent faster than that of the general population—has already surpassed by substantial measure the availability of adequate housing. Each of the public and private projects under construction or renovation that is planned to fill the real needs of the elderly quickly fills with tenants, and just as quickly forms a waiting list of hundreds. The demand for housing for the elderly will continue to grow, even more dramatically, in the years to come, and will represent an even greater challenge—and opportunity—for the professional housing manager.

Appendix A: Sources of Information

Institute of Real Estate Management

More than 6,000 professional property managers have met the stringent qualifying standards set by the Institute of Real Estate Management (IREM) in the areas of education, experience and ethical conduct. IREM grants these qualified professionals the designation CERTIFIED PROPERTY MANAGER® (CPM®), and invites them to participate in membership activities and benefits.

The Institute of Real Estate Management was founded in 1933 by a group of individuals concerned with establishing ethical standards of conduct for property management. IREM was organized as an affiliate of the National Association of Real Estate Boards, known today as the NATIONAL ASSOCIATION OF REALTORS®.

Firms engaged in property management which meet IREM's high standards in the areas of education, experience, integrity and financial stability earn the ACCREDITED MANAGEMENT ORGANIZATION® (AMO®) designation. AMO®s are full-service management firms providing maximum management services.

On-site residential managers demonstrating the required experience, education and ethical conduct can qualify for IREM's ACCREDITED RESIDENT MANAGER™ (ARM®) recognition.

In addition to identifying these professionals, IREM creates and sponsors a wide variety of courses, seminars and continuing education programs, nationally and locally. IREM's publishing program continually updates and adds to a library of technical journals, textbooks, cassettes, reprints, research studies and newsletters.

IREM members use their expertise to benefit the general public, other real estate professions and government housing agencies. Many CPM®s teach at local universities, serve on legislative committees, and assist government agencies in solving housing problems—in addition to practicing their professions. The U.S. Department of Housing and Urban Development has awarded IREM a special certificate of merit for the educational programs conducted for HUD officials. The Department of Energy has commended IREM for its extensive studies on the effects of energy conservation in income-producing properties. IREM has also worked with the National Bureau of Standards.

IREM committees have focused on topics such as rent control, national housing programs and government policies regarding energy conservation.

CPM®s manage more than 500 billion dollars' worth of real estate assets in the United States. They manage all types of income-producing property in the United States and Canada.

Information is available from IREM's staff on all aspects of property management—including hiring needs. Persons interested in becoming certified as professionals in the property management field can learn the steps to be taken in acquiring the needed credentials by contacting IREM. To reach IREM's national headquarters, phone (312) 661-1930, or write to:

Institute of Real Estate Management
430 North Michigan Avenue
Chicago, IL 60611-4090

Other Sources of Information

Administration on Aging
Office of Human Development Services
Department of Health and Human Services
200 Independence Ave., S.W.
Washington, DC 20201

American Association of Retired Persons
1909 K St., N.W.
Washington, DC 20049

American Council of the Blind
1211 Connecticut Ave., N.W.
Washington, DC 20036

American Council of Life Insurance
277 Park Ave.
New York, NY 10017

American Foundation for the Blind
15 W. 16th St.
New York, NY 10011

American Humane Association
Administrator of Special Programs
P.O. Box 1266
Denver, CO 80201

American Institute of Architects
1735 New York Ave.
Washington, DC 20006

American Longevity Association
1000 W. Carson St.
Torrance. CA 90509

American Speech and Hearing Association
9030 Old Georgetown Rd.
Washington, DC 20014

Architectural and Transportation Barriers
Compliance Board
330 C St., S.W.
Washington, DC 20202

Center for Independent Living
318 E. 15th St.
New York, NY 10013

Disabled American Veterans
3725 Alexandria Pike
Cole Spring, KY 41076

Gerontological Society of America
1835 K St., N.W.
Washington, DC 20006

Gray Panthers (national office)
3635 Chestnut St.
Philadelphia, PA 19104

Guiding Eyes for the Blind
Yorktown Heights, NY 10598

Institute of Rehabilitation Medicine
New York University Medical Center
400 E. 34th St.
New York, NY 10016

Medicaid and Medicare: for information, write—
Health Care Financing Administration
U.S. Department of Health and Human Services
200 Independence Ave., S.W.
Washington, DC 20201

Metropolitan Center for Independent Living, Inc.
1728 University Ave.
St. Paul, MN 55104

National Association of Area Agencies on Aging
600 Maryland Ave., S.W.
Washington, DC 20024

National Association of County Aging Programs
440 First St., N.W.
Washington, DC 20001

National Association of the Deaf
814 Thayer Ave.
Silver Spring, MD 20910

The National Association of Housing and Redevelopment
Officials
2600 Virginia Ave., N.W.
Washington, DC 20037

National Association of the Physically Handicapped
6473 Grandville Ave.
Detroit, MI 48228

National Association for Retarded Citizens
1522 K St., N.W.
Washington, DC 20005

National Blindness Information Center
National Federation of the Blind
1346 Connecticut Ave., N.W.
Washington, DC 20036

National Center for a Barrier-Free Environment
8401 Connecticut Ave., N.W.
Washington, DC 20015

National Council on the Aging, Inc.
600 Maryland Ave., S.W.
West Wing 100
Washington, DC 20024

National Council for Urban Economic Development
1730 K St., N.W.
Washington, DC 20006

National Fire Protection Association
Batterymarch Park
Quincy, MA 02269

National Institute on Aging
National Institutes of Health
9000 Rockville Pike
Bethesda, MD 20205

National Paraplegia Foundation
333 N. Michigan Ave.
Chicago, IL 60601

North Carolina Department of Insurance
The Special Office for the Handicapped
P.O. Box 26387
Raleigh, NC 27611

Paralyzed Veterans of America
7315 Wisconsin Ave., N.W.
Washington, DC 20014

President's Committee on Employment of the Handicapped
1111 Twentieth St., N.W.
Washington, DC 20036

Rehabilitation Services Administration
330 C St., S.W.
Washington, DC 20201

Security Equipment Industry Association (SEIA)
2665 30th St.
Santa Monica, CA 90405

The Seeing Eye, Inc.
P.O. Box 375M
Washington Valley Rd.
Morristown, NJ 07960

Sensory Aids Foundation
399 Sherman Ave.
Palo Alto, CA 94306

Sister Kenny Institute
Chicago Ave. at 27th St.
Minneapolis, MN 55407

Social Security Administration
U.S. Department of Health and Human Services
6401 Security Blvd.
Baltimore, MD 21235

Superintendent of Documents
Government Printing Office
North Capitol and H Sts., N.W.
Washington, DC 20401

U.S. Department of Housing and Urban Development
451 Seventh St., S.W.
Washington, DC 20410

Veterans Administration
810 Vermont Ave.
Washington, DC 20420

Appendix B: Support Services and Products

The following is a list of support services and products that can be useful in the management of housing for the elderly. The list is not meant to be exhaustive, but may serve as a convenient starting-point in building up a file for reference. It should be understood that inclusion in the list does not constitute endorsement by the author or by the Institute of Real Estate Management.

Consult the Yellow Pages, starting with the entries under "Aging," to find the service providers designated by the state under Title III of the Older Americans Act. Also use the Yellow Pages to find local providers of Food Stamps, Meals on Wheels, National Nutrition Program for the Elderly, HUD, Social Security, and the local offices of national organizations such as the Small Business Administration. Many cities and towns publish "Access" booklets, giving information about local buildings that provide supportive features for disabled persons. These listings include commercial establishments. An example is: *Access Chicago: A Resource Guide for the Physically Handicapped of Chicago.* This guide is published by the Rehabilitation Institute of Chicago, 345 E. Superior St., Chicago, IL 60611.

Sources	Services/Products	Sources	Services/Products
ACTION 806 Connecticut Ave., N.W. Washington, DC 20036	Foster Grandparent Program, Retired Senior Volunteer Program (RSVP), Senior Companion Program, Volunteers in Service to America (VISTA)	Administration on Aging Superintendent of Documents U.S. Government Printing Office North Capitol and H Sts., N.W. Washington, DC 20401	*Aging* magazine, films on aging

Sources	Services/Products
American Association of Homes for the Aging 1050 17th St., N.W. Washington, DC 20036	*AAHA News Scene, Housing Report, Washington Report*
American Association of Retired Persons 1909 K St., N.W. Washington, DC 20049	*Modern Maturity* magazine, restaurant guides
American Foundation for the Blind 15 W. 16th St. New York, NY 10011	Self-help/peer discussion guidebook and materials to identify and cope with loss of vision, hearing, memory
American Longevity Association 1835 K St., N.W. Washington, DC 20006	*Journal of Gerontology*
American National Standards Institute 1430 Broadway New York, NY 10018	Specifications for buildings and facilities
Ethel Percy Andrus Gerontology Center University of Southern California Los Angeles, CA 90024	Catalog of films about aging
Canadian Institute of Religion and Gerontology 296 Lawrence Ave. East Toronto, Ontario M4N 1T7 Canada	Newsletter
General Services Administration Public Buildings Service 18th and F Sts., S.W. Washington, DC 20405	Accessibility design criteria
International Council for Small Business St. Louis University Department of Management Sciences St. Louis, MO 63108	*Journal of Small Business Management, ICSB Newsletter*
International Society of Preretirement Planners Box 287 821 S. Gilbert St. Iowa City, IA 52244	*Active Times, Perspective*

Sources	Services/Products
Library of Congress Division for the Blind & Physically Handicapped 1291 Taylor St., N.W. Washington, DC 20542	Directory of Network Libraries and Machine Lending Agencies
National Association for the Deaf 5125 Radner Rd. Indianapolis, IN 46226	*Deaf American* magazine
National Association of the Deaf 814 Thayer Ave. Silver Spring, MD 10910	Publications, films, slides for training purposes
National Association of Retired Federal Employees 1533 New Hampshire Ave., N.W. Washington, DC 20036	*Retirement Life*
National Council on the Aging 600 Maryland Ave., S.W. Washington, DC 20024	*Perspective on Aging, Aging and Work, Current Literature on Aging, Senior Center Report*
National Easter Seal Society 2023 W. Ogden Ave. Chicago, IL 60612	Training programs, publications, audiovisuals
National Home-caring Council 67 Irving Pl. New York, NY 10003	Home health care services
National Resource Center for Consumer of Legal Services 1301 18th St., N.W. Washington, DC 20036	Guidance regarding legal counsel
National Retired Teachers Association 701 N. Montgomery St. Ojai, CA 93023	*NRTA Journal*
National Senior Citizens Law Center 1709 W. 8th St. Los Angeles, CA 90017	Counseling programs on legal matters

Sources	Services/Products	Sources	Services/Products
Senior Commmunity Service Employment Program Department of Labor 200 Constitution Ave., N.W. Washington, DC 20210	Subsidized community service employment opportunities	The Gerontological Society 1835 K St., N.W. Washington, DC 20006	*The Gerontologist* magazine
Sensory Aids Foundation 399 Sherman Ave. Palo Alto, CA 94306	*Sensory Aids Technology Update,* monthly newsletter	The Mennonite Board of Congregational Ministries Box 1245 Elkhart, IN 46515	Films on aging
Small Business Administration 1441 L St., N.W. Washington, DC 20416	Service Corps of Retired Executives (SCORE)		

Appendix C: Documents and Forms

Figure C.1.
Mei Lun Yuen: Elderly Rental
Application

MEI LUN YUEN 美鄰園
Elderly Rental Application 老人住戶申請表格

申請表格号碼
CERTIFICATE NUMBER_____

日期 DATE_____

你擁有汽車嗎， 多少部？
DO YOU OWN A CAR?____ HOW MANY?____

你想申請 單房單位 一睡房单位
ARE YOU APPLYING FOR STUDIO___, ONE BEDROOM___

申請人姓名
HEAD OF HOUSEHOLD (NAME)_____

生日日期
BIRTHDAY_____

配偶姓名
NAME OF SPOUSE_____

生日日期
BIRTHDAY_____

現址
PRESENT ADDRESS_____

現址居住年數
YEARS THERE_____

電話号碼
TELEPHONE NO._____

工作電話
(work)_____

住家電話
(home)_____

現址業主姓名
NAME OF CURRENT LANDLORD_____

電話号碼
PHONE NUMBER_____

業主地址
ADDRESS OF LANDLORD_____

前任業主姓名,地址
PREVIOUS LANDLORD_____
& ADDRESS

電話号碼
PHONE NUMBER_____

前址居住年數
NO. YEARS THERE_____

你有被迫遷過嗎。 有 沒有 有的話,請寫下該摟業主姓名丛地址
HAVE YOU EVER BEEN EVICTED? YES___, NO___. IF "YES" PLEASE GIVE LANDLORD NAME AND ADDRESS

SOURCE OF INCOME: 入息資料   Head of Household 申請人   Spouse 配偶

僱主姓名
NAME OF EMPLOYER   _____   _____

地址
ADDRESS   _____   _____

電話号碼
TELEPHONE NUMBER   _____   _____

職業
OCCUPATION

任職年數 年薪
YEARS EMPLOYED_____ ANNUAL WAGES_____

任職年數 年薪
YEARS EMPLOYED_____ ANNUAL WAGES_____

退休金 銀碼
SOCIAL SECURITY: AMOUNT $_____

户口号碼
ACCOUNT NUMBER_____

退休 殘廢 鰥寡
RETIREMENT$_____ DISABILITY$_____ WIDOW(ER)$_____

退休補助金 銀碼
SUPPLEMENTAL SECURITY INCOME: AMOUNT $_____

户口号碼
ACCOUNT NUMBER_____

年老 殘廢 失明
OLD AGE $_____ DISABILITY $_____ BLIND $_____

退役軍人補助金 銀碼
VETERAN'S BENEFITS: AMOUNT $_____

户口号碼
ACCOUNT NO._____

政府補助金 銀碼
PUBLIC ASSISTANCE: AMOUNT $_____

種類
TYPE_____

養老金 銀碼
PENSION: AMOUNT $_____

户口号碼
ACCOUNT NO._____

其他收入 銀碼
OTHER INCOME: AMOUNT $_____

户口号碼
ACCOUNT NO._____

ADDITIONAL COMMENTS: 附註

Figure C.1. (continued)

銀行戶口
BANK ACCOUNTS: 　　　　銀行名稱及地址　　　　　　　户口号碼
　　　　　　　　　　Name and Address of Banks　　　Account Number

Savings: 存摺戶口 _____　_____

　　　　　　　　　　　_____　_____

Checking: 支票戶口 _____　_____

LOANS AND/OR CHARGE ACCOUNTS: 貸款／信用咭

Name and Address 公司名稱及地址　　　每月遞還額　　　户口号碼
　　　　　　　　　　　　　　　　Monthly Payments　Account Number

_____　_____　_____

_____　_____　_____

_____　_____　_____

有自置物業否 (請詳述種類)
REAL ESTATE OWNED (Description/Type) _____

其他資產
OTHER ASSETS: _____

IN CASE OF EMERGENCY NOTIFY: (NAME) 姓名 _____ (ADDRESS) 地址 _____
緊急情況下, 可通知
　　　　　　　　(PHONE) 電話号碼 _____ , _____
　　　　　　　　醫生姓名
　　　　　　　　(Doctor's Name) _____
　　　　　　　　醫生電話
　　　　　　　　(Doctor's Phone No.) _____

你家內有殘廢者嗎?
ARE YOU OR ANY MEMBER OF YOUR FAMILY NOW LIVING WITH YOU HANDICAPPED? 有 YES___ , 沒有 NO___
有的話,是否需要特別照顧?　　　請述情況;
IF "YES", DO THEY REQUIRE SPECIAL ATTENTION? DESCRIBE: _____
你家內有成員需要醫生長期照顧否?
IS ANY MEMBER OF YOUR FAMILY UNDER A DOCTOR'S CONTINUOUS CARE? 有 YES___ , 沒有 NO___
你曾否或資料將被三藩市重建局追遷?
HAVE YOU BEEN DISPLACED OR DO YOU EXPECT TO BE DISPLACED BY THE SAN FRANCISCO REDEVELOPMENT
　　有　　　沒有　　有的話,請寫下現址;
AGENCY? YES___ , NO___ . If "yes" please give your present address: _____
你會講英文嗎?　會　　不會　你會講別國語言嗎?　　那國語言;
DO YOU SPEAK ENGLISH? YES___ , NO___ . DO YOU SPEAK ANOTHER LANGUAGE? WHICH ONE? _____
若不願答者,可免答此項問題.所得資料只是用作向聯邦及州政有報告.
THIS IS OPTIONAL: Information to be used for federal and state reporting purposes only.
　　　　　　印第安人　　　　　　黑人　　　　　菲律賓人　　　　　其他
　　RACE: American Indian ___　　Black ___　　Filipino ___　　Other ___
種族　　　亞洲人　　　　　　　白人　　　　　美籍西班牙人
　　　　　Asian ___　　　　　Caucasian ___　Spanish American ___

NOTE: The Management Company will make every effort to insure tenants' safety. However,
staff is neither equipped nor trained to handle major physical/medical problems.
Nor is the building equipped or staff expected to provide 24-hr monitoring of tenant.
Where applicable, alarm-system connections will be monitored to the best of
Management's ability under reasonable circumstances. Your signature below indicates
full knowledge and understanding of the foregoing.

Date _____　　Signature _____

註。本管理公司將盡量維護及保證住客的安全.在適當地方會安置警鐘
等設備。但住客若需要特別的照顧的話,本樓及本公司則未有任何
特別設備,故此不肯提供二十四小時的特別服務.請各住明白本公
司的立場,並在下面簽名以示閣下完全了解這個情況。

日期。_____　　簽名。_____

Figure C.2.
Indemnity-Guarantee
Agreement: An Example

Relating to _____
Apartment _____
In apartment building located at _____
Went to hospital on or about _____
Died on or about _____

Whereas the undersigned desired to obtain the personal effects and/or personal furnishings now on the premises rented by the lessee;

And, whereas, the undersigned represents to lessor that no administrator or executor has been appointed for the estate of the lessee;

Now, therefore, the undersigned does hereby agree as follows:

That the undersigned shall indemnify and hold harmless the said lessor from any claims, suits, actions, or litigation which may result as a consequence of the delivering of the aforesaid personal effects of the lessee by the lessor to the undersigned;

Dated this _____ day of _____ , 19 _____

_____ (Seal)

_____ (Seal)

Address: _____

City: _____

Phone: _____

Employed by _____

Address: _____

Figure C.3.
HUD Requirements: Excerpt
from Publication 4530.3

CHAPTER 2: HUD REQUIREMENTS REGARDING ELIGIBILITY FOR ASSISTANCE, TENANTS' RENTS AND UNIT SIZE

Section 1: Introduction to Chapter 2

2-1. *PURPOSE OF CHAPTER*. This Chapter details HUD requirements related to determination of Tenants' eligibility for assistance, calculation of Tenants' rents, and assignment of unit size. This Chapter relates only to applicants who wish to be admitted at an assisted rent. This Chapter does not discuss criteria for admission of unassisted Tenants (i.e., Tenants who will pay the HUD-approved market rent). Criteria for selecting Tenants from among the applicants found to meet HUD requirements, or the property management practices commonly used in screening and selecting Tenants are discussed in Chapter 3.

2-2. *OVERVIEW OF HUD REQUIREMENTS*. Before an applicant can be admitted at an assisted rent, management must determine that the HUD requirements listed below are met. Each of these requirements are explained in more detail in the remaining sections of this Chapter.

a. The applicant must be a family; a single person who is elderly, disabled, handicapped or displaced as defined by HUD: or a single person who is eligible pursuant to paragraph 2-4. (See Section 2.)

b. The applicant must have an Eligibility Income less than or equal to the HUD-established income limit. (See Sections 3 and 4.)

c. An appropriately sized unit must be available within the project. Units are assigned according to family size and composition. (See Section 5.)

d. The applicant must agree to pay the rent required by the formula used in the subsidy program under which the applicant will be admitted. (See Section 6.)

Section 2: Household Characteristics and Eligibility of Single Persons.

2-3. *DEFINITIONS OF HOUSEHOLD CHARACTERISTICS*. In evaluating an applicant's eligibility pursuant to paragraph 2-2a above, the Owner shall use the following definitions of elderly, handicapped, disabled and displaced.

a. *Elderly* means a family whose head, spouse or sole member is 62 years of age or older, handicapped or disabled as defined below. Elderly families also include two or more handicapped or disabled persons living together or one or more such persons living with another person who is essential to the elderly, handicapped or disabled person's care and well-being.

b. *Handicapped* means a person having a physical or mental impairment which: (1) is expected to be of long or indefinite duration; (2) substantially impedes his or her ability to live independently; and (3) is of such a nature that the person's ability to live independently could be improved by more suitable housing conditions.

c. *Disabled* refers to a person who is under a disability as defined in Section 223 of the Social Security Act or in Section 102(b)(5) of the Developmental Disabilities Services and Facilities Construction Amendments of 1970. Receipt of veteran's benefits for disability, whether service-oriented or otherwise, does not automatically establish disability. The Owner must make the determination based upon his/her evaluation of the applicant's condition.

(1) Section 223 of the Social Security Act defines disability as:

(a) "Inability to engage in any substantial gainful activity by reason of any medically determinable physical or mental impairment which can be expected to result in death or which has lasted or can be expected to last for a continuous period of not less than 12 months; or

(b) In the case of an individual who has attained the age of 55 and is blind (within the meaning of "blindness" as defined in Section 416 (i)(1) of this title), inability by reason of such blindness to engage in substantial gainful activity requiring skills or abilities comparable to those of any gainful activity in which he has previously engaged some regularity and over a substantial period of time."

(2) Section 102(b)(5) of the Developmental Disabilities Services and Facilities Construction Amendments of 1970 defines disability as:

"A disability attributable to mental retardation, cerebral palsy, epilepsy, or another neu-

Figure C.3. (continued)

rological condition of an individual found by the Secretary (of Health and Human Services) to be closely related to mental retardation or to require treatment similar to that required for mentally retarded individuals, which disability originates before such individual attains age eighteen, which has continued or can be expected to continue indefinitely, and which constitutes a substantial handicap to such individual."

d. *Displaced* refers to a person: 1) who has been displaced by governmental action; or 2) whose unit has been extensively damaged or destroyed as a result of a disaster, declared or otherwise formally recognized, pursuant to Federal disaster relief laws.

2-4. *ELIGIBILITY OF SINGLE PERSONS.* A single person is defined as a person who lives alone or intends to live alone and is not elderly, displaced or the remaining member of a Tenant family. *Elderly, disabled, handicapped or displaced persons or the remaining member of an existing Tenant household are eligible for any HUD assistance program.* Other single persons may be admitted at an assisted rent only in accordance with the criteria discussed in paragraph 2-4a and b.

a. *Section 8.* The U.S. Housing Act of 1937, as amended, restricts the admission of single persons in all Section 8 programs. In any Section 8 program, the Owner may admit single persons only after obtaining the prior written approval of HUD. HUD will generally approve requests under the following circumstances.

(1) The project is a low-income or lower-income project and is experiencing sustained vacancies and no eligible applicants other than single persons are available; or

(2) The project is one which has been, or is intended to be, converted to a low-income or lower-income project and:

(a) Single persons are residing in the project at the time of conversion; or

(b) The HUD Field Office determines that the project is not suitable for occupancy by small families or the elderly,

disabled, or handicapped because of design or location.

b. *Other Programs.* HUD does not restrict occupancy by single persons. Owners should select Tenants in accordance with their Tenant selection plans.

Section 3: Annual Income and Eligibility Income

2-5. *GENERAL.* Annual Income is the *gross* amount of income *anticipated* to be received by all *adult* members of the household during the twelve months following the effective date of the Certification or Recertification of Tenant Eligibility. The income to be received by minors is not included in Annual Income. The full definition of what is and is not included in Annual Income is set forth in Exhibits 2-1 and 2-2 at the end of this Chapter.

a. The income inclusions in Exhibit 2-1 are arranged in the same order as the income exclusions in Exhibit 2-2. If any category of income has elements which are excluded from Annual Income and others which are included in Income, the inclusions will be discussed in Exhibit 2-1 under the same number as the exclusions are discussed in Exhibit 2-2. For example, types of military pay which are included in Annual Income will be grouped under *Item No. 4* on Exhibit 2-1 and types of military pay excluded from Annual Income will be grouped under *Item No. 4* of Exhibit 2-2.

b. When an applicant indicates that he/she is receiving public assistance and verification efforts reveal that public assistance is specifically designated for shelter and utilities, the Project Owner must determine whether the amount of the grant is fixed or may vary according to the recipient's actual shelter and utilities cost. If the public assistance payment is computed on an actual cost basis, the amount of public assistance income to be included in Annual Income is:

(i) the total amount of the public assistance minus the amount specifically designated for shelter and utilities; plus

(ii) the maximum amount which the Public Assistance Agency could in fact allow the family for shelter and utilities.

Ed. note: 2-3d refers to single persons and families.

Figure C.4.
Medical History Card: An
Example

Tenant: _____

Fire department phone: _____

Doctor: _____ Office: _____ Home: _____

Relative to be notified: _____ Phone: _____

Clergyman: _____

Brief medical history: _____

_____

_____

List of medications: Location in apartment:

_____   _____

_____   _____

_____   _____

_____   _____

Figure C.5.
Medical Report: A Two-Part
Example

TO PHYSICIAN: (Name of housing complex) is a housing development for well elderly persons 62 years of age or older or handicapped or developmentally disabled persons 18 years of age or older. Staff will be available 24 hours a day on each call for help in an emergency. A Medical Report on each applicant is required. Please complete this form and mail it to the above address. Thank you.

—The Management

PART 1

Applicant's signature and date:

Name of applicant (please type or print):

Applicant's address:

Street and number, city, state, zip:

Medical history

Diabetes?	Seizures?
Dizziness?	Arthritis?
GVA?	Heart disease?
Other?	

Dates of hospitalization for illness or surgery:

Mental illness

Dates of hospitalization for mental illness:

Type of mental illness:

Results:

Present mental condition:

History of drug addiction or alcoholism:

Allergies and sensitivities to drugs:

Laboratory: date and result of—

Chest X ray:
EKG:
Urinalysis:

Sp. Gr.:	Al.:
Sug.:	Micro.:

Hematocrit or CBC:

Physical examination

Blood pressure:	Pulse:
Height:	Weight:

Present condition of—

Eyes:	Skin:
Vision:	Throat:
Hearing:	Lungs:
Heart:	Breasts:
Abdomen:	
Extremities and joints:	
Peripheral arteries:	
Locomotion:	
Incontinence: Urine?	Feces?

PART 2

Treatment

Special diet?	Type:
Medication:	Dosage:
Other:	

Ambulation

Unassisted?	With walker?
With personal help?	
With cane?	With wheelchair?
Not at all?	

Evaluation of applicant's ability to adjust to this housing

Does this applicant need assistance to—
1. Bathe and dress?
2. Care for apartment?
3. Prepare meals?
4. Walk outdoors in fair weather?
5. Handle personal finances?
6. Remember apt. no., phone no., name of nearest relative?

Does this applicant—
1. Drive a car?
2. Get along well with others?
3. Have interests, friends outside own apartment?

Diagnosis and summary of needs

Physician's signature:

Physician's address, phone number and date:

Figure C.6.
Mental Status Questionnaire

Please write interviewee's own words. If there is any question about correctness, give no hints. Repeat question as often as necessary, but do not rephrase. (Adapted with permission from Goldfarb-Kahn-Pollack test.)

1. What is the name (address) of this place?
   (name of housing complex or hospital, street address)

2. Where is it?
   (city, state)

3. What is today's date?
   (Day of the week is not acceptable.)

4. Month?

5. Year?

6. How old are you?
   (If records indicate birthdate is uncertain, credit if estimate is within two years of age given by family.)

7. When were you born? Month?

8. Year?

9. Who is the president of the United States?

10. Who was president before him?

Comments:

Score

0–2 errors (no or mild impairment)
3–8 errors (moderately advanced impairments)
9–10 errors (severe brain dysfunction)

Figure C.7.
Independent Living
Capabilities: 20 Critical
Factors

I: Independent

1. Able to prepare adequate meals independently. Eats without assistance.
2. Maintains home alone or with occasional help with heavy work.
3. Is mobile without any aids, can walk 6 to 8 blocks and climb stairs without assistance.
4. Toilet-cares for self at toilet completely. No incontinence.
5. Medications—is responsible for taking medications in correct dosages at correct times without assistance.
6. Has little or no difficulty with time, place, person orientation (Goldfarb-Kahn-Pollack test).
7. Able to fully participate in planning and exercises good judgment in decision making or substantially intact—capable of participating in planning and decision making with minor dependence on others.
8. Apparently free of anxiety, depression, phobias, paranoia, or symptoms may be present in mild form but do not significantly hinder daily functioning.
9. Use of drugs or alcohol is not abusive.
10. Is aware of and practices routine safety measures without reminders or teaching assistance.
11. Obtains own groceries and other items needed for daily living.
12. Manages financial matters independently (budgets, writes and cashes checks, pays rent and bills, goes to bank, collects and keeps track of income).
13. Travels independently on public transportation or drives own car or arranges own travel via taxi but does not otherwise use public transportation.
14. Bathing: bathes self (tub, shower, sponge bath) without help.
15. Dressing: dresses, undresses and selects clothes from own wardrobe with no or very minor assistance.
16. Grooming: (Neatness, hair, nails, hands, face, clothing) always neatly dressed, well groomed without assistance.
17. Free of disturbing, disabling character traits, personal habits; grooming and dress reflect good hygiene and interest in personal appearance, or mildly disturbing character traits which would not significantly impair capacity for group living, acceptable personal habits and hygiene.
18. Maintains satisfactory relationships with family, friends and other residents. May be becoming less active in sustaining them.
19. Is able to speak and hear, read and write with little or no difficulty.
20. Able to dial and converse over the telephone—able to look up numbers.

II: Independent with supportive services

1. Requires health aide/homemaker, family or friends to prepare adequate meals on periodic or short term basis. Eats with minor assistance and may be untidy.
2. Performs light daily tasks but cannot maintain acceptable level of cleanliness without chore service/homemaker. Assistance is available and accepted.
3. Is mobile with mechanical aids (wheelchair, cane, crutches, walker, braces) and/or occasional available assistance. Able to go in and out of wheelchair without assistance.
4. Needs reminders about or minor and occasional assistance with toilet/personal care. May soil or wet while asleep more than once every two weeks.
5. At times confused by medications and requires periodic supervision of dosages. Supervision available and accepted.
6. Has intermittent or moderate confusion in time, place, person orientation.
7. Occasional memory lapses. May have always had limited intellectual capacities. Can participate in planning but may be slow in grasping content or need support from others in decision making.
8. May have mildly disturbing or mildly disabling anxiety, depression, phobias, paranoia.
9. Is developing a pattern of drug and/or alcohol abuse. Has not caused disturbances, accepts assistance.
10. Routine safety measures: requires some teaching assistance initially, but functions satisfactorily with no further assistance.
11. Obtains own food and other necessary items with some assistance from others. Assistance is available.
12. Manages some day-to-day purchases but needs help with banking and major purchases. May have or need conservator.
13. Travels on public transportation when assisted by others or travels limited to taxi or automobile with assistance of others. Occasionally requires others to make transportation arrangements for them. Assistance is available.
14. Bathes self with help in getting in and out of tub, shower; or washes face and hands only but cannot bathe rest of body. Accepts available assistance of family, friends or health aide/homemaker to bathe rest of body.
15. Needs moderate assistance in dressing, undressing and selection of clothes. Assistance is available and accepted.
16. Grooms self adequately with help of hygiene education and/or assistance. May need moderate assistance on short-term basis. Assistance is available and accepted.

Figure C.7.   (continued)

17. Mildly disturbing character traits which are not too disabling. Continues to have interest in appearance and maintains acceptable hygiene with some supervision (available and accepted).

18. May have had adequate interpersonal relationships in the past, but currently shows diminution of interest or minor to moderate problems with this sphere. May require occasional encouragement and/or stimulation. May be developing a pattern of difficulty with interpersonal relationships, including family and other residents.

19. Is able to speak and hear or read and write. May have moderate difficulty and may use electronic or mechanical aids.

20. Uses phone with difficulty. May only dial a few well-known numbers. May need electronic aid.

III: Supported living situation required

1. Requires extensive assistance with all meals or refuses to prepare or eat adequate meals. Totally dependent on health aide/homemaker/family or friends for preparation of adequate meals. Refuses assistance, or assistance is not available.

2. Needs help with all home maintenance tasks. Does not participate in any housekeeping tasks or refuses assistance in maintaining acceptable level of cleanliness, or assistance is not available.

3. Requires extensive assistance on a regular basis to carry out routine living functions—in and out of wheelchair, bed, toilet, dressing. Refuses assistance, or assistance is not available.

4. Soils or wets while awake more than once a week or has no control over bladder or bowels.

5. Requires daily or excessive supervision of medications for more than short period of time. Refuses supervision, or supervision is not readily available.

6. Severely disoriented in regard to time, place and person.

7. Requires considerable help from others in planning and decision making. Memory disorientation is sufficient to warrant daily or around-the-clock nursing care and supervision. Totally dependent on others for planning.

8. May have moderate to severe disturbing or disabling anxiety, depression, phobias, paranoia. Possibility of danger to self and others.

9. Frequently under the influence of drugs and/or alcohol and displays disruptive behavior. Does not maintain own health and apartment. Refuses assistance.

10. Refuses to practice safety measures or is frequently unaware of normal safety precautions.

11. Cannot or will not obtain food and other necessary items. Refuses assistance, or assistance is not available.

12. Incapable of handling financial matters. Has or needs guardian. Refuses assistance, or assistance is not available.

13. Requires extensive assistance with transportation or help in obtaining transportation for medical/dental appointments. Does not or will not travel, or adequate transportation is not available.

14. Cannot or will not wash self. Refuses assistance, or assistance is not available.

15. Needs major assistance with dressing, and such assistance is not available.

16. Needs regular assistance, or supervision in grooming. Refuses assistance, or assistance is not available.

17. Moderately to severely disturbing character traits. Requires considerable supervision and assistance for personal grooming. Incapable of conforming to socially acceptable standards of personal hygiene. Character traits create severe problems in management.

18. Needs considerable to excessive encouragement and/or stimulation. Interest and concern with regard to others has diminished. May be unable to maintain more than minimal personal relationship.

19. Has severe impairments of communication faculties. Has excessive difficulty in understanding and being understood. Refuses assistance, or assistance is not available.

20. Does not use telephone, or refuses to have phone even though it is necessary for health and safety.

Figure C.8.
Critical and Contributory
Factors: A Form

Mark one of the following ratings for each factor:

I: **Independent**
II: **Independent with Support**
III: **Needs Support**

Critical and Contributory Factors	Rating	Comments
Personal Adjustment		
Personal Care		
Bathing		
Dressing		
Grooming		
Toilet		
Medication		
Alcohol, Drugs (Use/Abuse)		
Group Living Capability		
Communication Capabilities		
Mental Functioning		
Time/Place/Person Orientation		
Use of Telephone		
Routine Safety Awareness		
Mobility		
Housekeeping		
Meal Preparation/Diet		
Shopping Capabilities		
Transportation		
Financial		

Bibliography

Accessible Housing. Raleigh, N.C.: Special Office for the Handicapped, Insurance Commissioner's Office, North Carolina Department of Insurance, 1980.

Adaptations and Techniques for the Disabled Homemaker. Minneapolis, Minn.: Sister Kenny Institute: n.d.

"Altering Homes for Aging Americans." Washington, D.C.: The Urban Institute *Policy and Research Report*, 13 (1) (Winter 1983).

Barach, Jerry. "Aid to the Elderly Fund." *The Israel Economist* 39 (August 1983): 36.

Barrier-Free Site Design. Washington, D.C.: American Society of Landscape Architects Foundation: n.d.

Bell, T. E. *Technologies for the Handicapped and the Aged.* Washington, D.C.: Government Printing Office, 1979.

Birren, James E. "Aging in America: Roles for Psychology." *American Psychologist* (March 1983): 298–299.

Birren, James E., and Schaie, K. Warner (eds.). *Handbook of the Psychology of Aging.* New York: Van Nostrand Reinhold, 1977.

Birren, James E., and Sloane, R. Bruce (eds.). *Handbook of Aging and Mental Health.* Englewood Cliffs, N.J.: Prentice Hall, 1980.

Brown, Robert N.; Atto, Clifford B.; Freeman, Alan D.; and Netzorg, Gordon W. *The Rights of Older Persons: The Basic ACLU Guide to an Older Person's Rights.* New York: Avon Books, 1979.

Bruck, Lilly. *Access—The Guide to a Better Life for Disabled Americans.* New York: Random House, 1978.

Cary, Jane Randolph. *How to Create Interiors for the Disabled.* New York: Pantheon, 1978.

Chartbook on Aging in America. Washington, D.C.: GPO, n.d.

Chasin, Joseph. *Home in a Wheelchair.* Washington, D.C.: Paralyzed Veterans of America, n.d.

Chellis, R. D.; Seagle, J. F.; and Seagle, B. *Congregate Housing for Older People.* Lexington, Mass.: Lexington Books, 1982.

Clark, John G., et al. *Three Generations in Twentieth Century America.* rev. ed. Homewood, Ill.: The Dorsey Press, 1982.

Collins, Carole J. L. *Social Service Needs of the Aged.* Chicago: University of Chicago School of Social Service Administration, Center for the Study of Welfare Policy, 1972.

Davis, Linda J., and Broday, Elaine M. *Rape and Older Women: A Guide to Prevention and Protection.* Washington, D.C.: GPO, 1979.

Determinants of Institutionalization of the Aged. Washington, D.C.: The Urban Institute, Research Report No. 10-009, n.d.

Diamond, Marion C. "Aging and Cell Loss: Calling for an Honest Count." *Psychology Today* (Sept. 1976): 126.

Donahue, W. T.; Thompson, M. M.; and Current, D. J. *Congregate Housing for Older People.* Washington, D.C.: GPO, 1977.

Eisdorfer, Carl. "Conceptual Models of Aging." *American Psychologist* (February 1983): 197–202.

"Elderly Tell at Hearing How Drugs Abuse Them." *Chicago Tribune* (June 1, 1983): n.p.

Fact Book on Aging. Washington, D.C.: National Council on the Aging, annual.

Federal Benefits for Veterans and Dependents. Washington, D.C. GPO, annual.

Gelwicks, L. E. "Plan Joins Nursing Home to Nursery School." *Modern Nursing Home* 28 (1972): 47–49.

Gelwicks, L. E. and Newcomer, R. J. *Planning Housing Environments for the Elderly.* Washington, D.C.: National Council on the Aging, 1974.

Glosscote, Raymond; Gudeman, Jon E., and Miles, Donald. *Creative Mental Health Services for the Elderly.* Washington, D.C.: American Psychiatric Association, 1977.

Golant, Stephen M. *Location and Environment of Elderly Population.* New York: John Wiley & Sons, 1979.

————, "Residential Concentrations of the Future Elderly." *The Gerontologist.* Supplement. (February 1975).

"Golden Dreams." *Chicago Sun-Times* Retirement Living Section (July 1, 1983).

Green, Isaac, et al. *Housing for the Elderly: The Development and Design Process.* New York: Van Nostrand Reinhold, 1975.

Harkness, Sarah P., and Groom, James N. *Building Without Barriers for the Disabled.* New York: Whitney Library of Design, 1976.

Hartman, Chester; Horovitz, Jerry; and Herman, Robert. "Designing with the Elderly: A User Needs Survey for Housing Low-Income Senior Citizens." *The Gerontologist* 16 (4) (1976): n.p.

Himber, Louis L. *Dollars and Sense After 60.* New York: Federation of Protestant Welfare Agencies, n.d.

Housing for a Maturing Population. Washington, D.C.: Urban Land Institute, Urban Institute Press, 1983.

"How to Meet Housing Demand." *Modern Maturity* (August–September 1983): 82.

Howard, Edward F. "Jobs for Older People." *American Psychologist* (March 1983): 319–322.

Howell, S. C. *Designing for Aging: Patterns of Use.* Cambridge, Mass.: MIT Press, 1980.

Huff, Robert I. *National Directory of Retirement Facilities.* 3 vols. Washington, DC: The American Association of Retired Persons and National Retired Teachers Association, annual.

Huttman, Elizabeth. "Multi-Level Care Facilities for the Elderly in Denmark and Holland." *Housing and Society* 9 (1) (1982): 20–30.

"If You Live to Be 100—It Won't Be Unusual." *U.S. News & World Report* (May 9, 1983): A-10.

Ittig, Kathleen Browne and Spencer, Barbara Brandi. "Consumer Economics of Property Tax Policy for Senior Citizens: Needs Assessment Phase." *Housing and Society* 9 (1) (1982): 42–47.

Keith-Ross, J. *Old People, New Lives: Community Creation in a Retirement Residence.* Chicago: University of Chicago Press, 1977.

Kelley, Edward N. *Practical Apartment Management.* 2d ed. Chicago: Institute of Real Estate Management, 1981.

Kotulak, Ronald. "Can We Live to Age 120?" *Chicago Tribune* Section 5 (May 4, 1983): 1, 2.

Lareau, Leslie S. "Relocation of the Elderly: A Social Context for Stress." *Housing and Society,* 9 (1) (1982): 3–10.

Laurie, Gini. *Housing and Home Services for the Disabled: Guidelines and Experiences in Independent Living.* Hagerstown, Maryland: Harper and Row, 1977.

Lawton, M. P. *Environment and Aging.* Monterey, Calif.: Brooks-Cole Publishing, 1980.

———, *Planning and Managing Housing for the Elderly.* New York: Wiley-Interscience, 1975.

Lawton, M. P.; Greenbaum, M.; and Liebowitz, B. "The Lifespan of Housing Environments for the Aging." *The Gerontologist* 20 (1980): 56–64.

Lawton, M. P., and Hoover, S. L. (eds.). *Community Housing Choices for Older Americans.* New York: Springer Publishing, 1981.

Lawton, M. P.; Newcomer, R. J.; and Byerts, T. O. (eds.). *Community Planning for an Aging Society.* Stroudsburg, Penn.: Dowden Hutchinson Ross, 1976.

Lazarus, Richard S., and DeLongis, Anita. "Psychological Stress and Coping in Aging." *American Psychologist* (March 1983): 245–254.

Leifer, I. "Normal Elderly in the Community: Technology Leading to New and Improved Products." Paper presented at the National Research Conference on Technology and Aging, Racine, Wis., 1981.

Leuking, F. Dean. *A Century of Caring.* St. Louis, Mo.: The Board of Social Ministry, The Lutheran Church-Missouri Synod, 1968.

Life-Care Industry 1983. Philadelphia, Penn.: Laventhol & Horwath, 1983.

Low Rise Housing for Older People—Behavioral Criteria for Design. Washington D.C.: GPO, 1977.

Managing Housing & Services for the Elderly. New York: The National Center for Housing Management, 1977.

Marty, Martin E., and Vaux, Kenneth L. (eds.). *Health/Medicine and the Faith Traditions.* Philadelphia, Pa.: Fortress Press, 1982.

Masel, Deborah. "New Vistas for the Elderly." *The Israel Economist* 39 (August 1983): 37.

Mason, John M. *The Fourth Generation.* Minneapolis, Minn.: Augsburg Press, 1978.

McGaugh, James L. "Preserving the Presence of the Past—Hormonal Influences on Memory Storage." *American Psychologist* (February 1983): 161–174.

Mealtime Manual for the Aged and Handicapped. New York: New York University Medical Center, Institute of Rehabilitation Medicine: n.d.

Miller, A. H.; Gurin, P.; and Gurin, G. "Age Consciousness and Political Mobilization of Older Americans." Paper presented at the 32nd annual meeting of the Gerontological Society, Washington, D.C., November, 1979.

National Institutes of Health. *Special Report on Aging,* 1979, p. 2.

Neighborhood Services for the Aging—A Neighborhood Action Guide. Washington, D.C.: Civic Action Institute, 1979.

Neugarten, Bernice L. "Age Groups in American Society and the Rise of the Young-Old." *Annals of the American Academy* (1974): 187–198.

———, "Health Care, Medicare, and Health Policy for Older People—A Conversation with Arthur Flemming." *American Psychologist* (March 1983): 311–315.

————, (ed.). *Middle Age and Aging.* Chicago: University of Chicago Press, 1973.

Newman, S. J. "Housing Adjustments of the Disabled Elderly." *The Gerontologist* 16 (1976): 312–317.

Norback, Craig and Peter. *Older American's Handbook.* New York: Van Nostrand Reinhold, 1977.

Obenland, Robert J. *Design Options for a Continuum of Care Environment.* Concord, New Hampshire: New England Non-Profit Housing Development Corporation, 1976.

"Officials Fight to Let Elderly Keep Pets in Federal Assisted Housing." *Wall Street Journal* (May 4, 1983): n.p.

Oppeneer, Joan E., and Vervoren, Thora M. *Gerontological Pharmacology/A Resource for Health Practitioners.* St. Louis, Mo.: C. V. Mosby Co., 1983.

"Options of Older Workers: To Retire or Not to Retire." Washington, D.C.: The Urban Institute *Policy and Research Report* 13 (1) (Winter 1983): 1–3.

Pagliaro, Louis A., and Pagliaro, Ann M. *Pharmacologic Aspects of Aging.* St. Louis, Mo.: C. V. Mosby Co., 1983.

Pastalan, Leon and Carson, Daniel H. (eds.). *Spatial Behavior of Older People.* Ann Arbor, Mich.: The University of Michigan–Wayne State University Institute of Gerontology, 1970.

Pepper, Claude. "Social Security—The Challenge of the 1980s." *American Psychologist* (March 1983): 308–310.

Percy, Charles H. *Growing Old in the Country of the Young—with a Practical Resource Guide for the Aged and their Families.* New York: McGraw-Hill Book Co., 1974.

Peterson, J. S.; Hamovitch, N.; and Larsen, A. H. *Housing Needs and Satisfactions of the Elderly.* Los Angeles: Ethel Percy Andrus Gerontology Center, University of California, 1973.

President's Committee on Employment of the Handicapped. *A Handbook on the Legal Rights of Handicapped People.* GPO, n.d.

President's Committee on Employment of the Handicapped. *Careers for the Homebound—Home Study Educational Opportunities.* GPO: n.d.

Regnier, V. (ed.). *Planning for the Elderly—Alternative Community Analysis Techniques.* Los Angeles: University of California Press, 1979.

Salisbury, Paul Allen, and Beer, Rose S. "Social Segregation: Barriers to Mobility in Urban Domiciliary Care." *Housing and Society* 9 (1) (1982).

Shear, Mel A. *Handbook of Building Maintenance Management.* Reston, Va.: Reston Publishing Co., 1983.

Sherman, S. R. "The Choice of Retirement Housing Among the Well-Elderly." *Aging and Human Development* 2 (1971): n.p.

Silverstone, Barbara, and Hyman, Helen Kandel. *You & Your Aging Parent.* New York: Pantheon Books, 1982.

Skinner, B. F. "Intellectual Self-Management in Old Age." *American Psychologist* (March 1983): 239–244.

Skinner, B. F., and Vaughan, M. E. *Enjoy Old Age: A Program of Self-Management.* New York: W. W. Morrow and Company, 1983.

Slavik, J. Ronald. "Senior Housing: Practical Innovations." Chicago: Institute of Real Estate Management. *Journal of Property Management* (July/August 1981): 229–231.

Smith, Tilman R. *In Favor of Growing Older.* Scottdale, Pa.: Herald Press, 1981.

Soldo, Beth J. "America's Elderly in the 1980s." Washington, D.C.: Population Reference Bureau, *Population Bulletin* 35 (4) (November 1980).

Specifications for Making Buildings and Facilities Accessible to and Usable by Physically Handicapped People. ANSI AN117.1. New York: American National Standards Institute, 1980.

Steinfeld, E. "Designing Adaptable Housing to Meet Barrier-Free Goals." *Architectural Record* (March 1980): 57–61.

Storandt, Martha. "Psychology's Response to the Graying of America." *American Psychologist* (March 1983): 323–326.

Struyk, R. F. *The Housing and Neighborhood Environment of the Elderly: Challenges for the 1980s*. Washington, D.C.: The Urban Institute, 1981.

———, "The Housing Situation of Elderly Americans." *The Gerontologist* 17 (1977): 130–139.

Struyk, R. F., and Soldo, Beth F. *Improving the Elderly's Housing: A Key to Preserving the Nation's Housing Stock and Neighborhoods*. Cambridge, Mass.: Ballinger Publishing Co., 1980.

Substitute or Supplement: Day Care for the Elderly. Washington, D.C.: The Urban Institute, Research Report No. 70-005, n.d.

Sumichrast, Michael; Shafer, Ronald; and Sumichrast, Marika. *Where Will You Live Tomorrow?* Homewood, Ill.: Dow Jones-Irwin, 1981.

Swenson, Clifford H. "A Respectable Old Age." *American Psychologist* (March 1983): 327–334.

"Taking Down the Barriers." Chicago: National Easter Seal Society, distributors. *Journal of American Insurance* (Spring 1982): 11–17.

Tanner, Ronald. "Housing the Gray Wave/Retirement Centers Offer Care for the Elderly." *Venture* (March 1983): 74, 76.

The Community Handbook. New York: Center for Independent Living, n.d.

The On-Site Housing Manager's Resource Book—Housing for the Elderly. Washington, D.C.: The National Center for Housing Management, 1974.

The Wheelchair in the Kitchen. Washington, D.C.: Paralyzed Veterans of America, n.d.

Thorpe, Norman. "Communities for Retirees on Rise Again." *Wall Street Journal* (September 2, 1983): 13, 24.

Tolliver, Lennie-Mae. "Social and Mental Health Needs of the Aged." *American Psychologist* (March 1983): 316–318.

U.S. Congress. Senate. *Developments in Aging*. GPO, annual.

U.S. Congress. House. *Families: Aging and Changing*. GPO, annual.

U.S. Government Printing Office (GPO)
Superintendent of Documents
North Capitol and H Sts., N.W.
Washington, D.C. 20402

Vandenbos, Gary R., and Buchanan, Joan. "Aging, Research on Aging, and National Policy." *American Psychologist* (March 1983): 300–307.

Varro, Barbara. "Middle Age at 70?" *Chicago Sun-Times* (March 23, 1983): 49, 51.

Vocational and Educational Opportunities for the Disabled. Albertson, N.Y.: Insurance Company of North America and Human Resources Center, n.d.

Volinsky, Joan. "Research Crumbles Stereotypes of Aging." Washington, D.C.: *APA Monitor* (American Psychological Association) 8 (August, 1983): 26–28.

Wachs, M. *Transportation for the Elderly: Changing Lifestyles, Changing Needs*. Berkeley, Calif.: University of California Press, 1979.

Weiss, Joseph Douglas. *Better Buildings for the Aged*. New York: Hopkinson and Blake, 1969.

Wheelchair Bathrooms. Washington, D.C.: Paralyzed Veterans of America, n.d.

Wilner, M. A.; Pease, V. A.; and Walgren, R. S. (eds.). *Planning & Financing Facilities for the Elderly*. Washington, D.C.: American Association of Homes for the Aging, 1978.

Wood, Elizabeth. *The Beautiful Beginnings/The Failure to Learn: Fifty Years of Public Housing in America*. Washington, D.C.: National Center for Housing Management, 1982.

Index

IREM
Property Management
Library